Nonverbal Language Integration
for
Exercising Vagus Nerve Pathways

Introducing the Theory and Practice of
Enhancing Rapport through Pragmatics

Dorothy Bohntinsky

Dorothy Bohntinsky
In-Word Bound Publishing

Note to readers:
This volume is intended as a general information resource for professionals practicing in healthcare related fields. The intention is not to suggest a new standard in clinical practice or an evidenced-based practice therapy technique or strategy. The purpose is to introduce a new theory and exercises for enhancing rapport with clients and family through nonverbal language. While the author/publisher cannot guarantee the complete accuracy, efficacy, and appropriateness of any particular recommendation in every aspect, great care was taken to apply evidence-based-practice standards and ethical practices throughout this volume. The author is not rendering professional wellness advice to the reader. The ideas and approaches contained in this book do not substitute for consulting a physician on all matters of physical and mental health.

Dorothy Bohntinsky
In-Word Bound Publishing
25890 Fairview Ave.
Hayward, CA 94542

Printed in the United States of America
First edition.

Library of Congress Cataloging-in-Publication Data
Bohntinsky, Dorothy
    Nonverbal language integration for exercising vagus nerve pathways:
    the theory and practice of enhancing outcomes through pragmatics/
    Dorothy Bohntinsky/ 1st ed.
    Includes bibliographical references and index.
    LCCN 2019916124

ISBN 978-1-7341406-0-6

This guidebook is dedicated to my grandchildren:
Kerrigan, Gregor, and Conrad.

Their willingness to participate in early experiments
is what inspired me to ask questions and do research.
Their insistence that I document the discoveries
so they could read them one day
is what inspired me to write down the answers.
My observations of improved rapport,
which coincided with doing the exercises,
is what inspired me to publish this guidebook.

TABLE OF CONTENTS

PREFACE   vii

Chapter One: A SPORTS COLLAR DOES WHAT!?   1

Chapter Two: LOOKING FOR CLUES   5

Chapter Three: FROM INFORMAL EXPLORATION TO A HYPOTHESIS   11

Chapter Four: HOW DOES JUGULAR COMPRESSION   15
              IMPROVE MOOD AND FOCUS?

Chapter Five: EXPLORING THE FUNCTIONS OF THE VAGUS NERVE   21

Chapter Six: THE CRANIAL NERVES OF SOCIAL ENGAGEMENT   33

Chapter Seven: THE VENTRAL VAGUS NERVE AND RAPPORT   39

Chapter Eight: THE COMPLEXITY OF THE YAWN   45

Chapter Nine: INTUITION   53

Chapter Ten: THE SWALLOW AND NEUROPLASTICITY   57

Chapter Eleven: ASSESSING AND INNERVATING THE VAGUS NERVE   65

Chapter Twelve: THE THEORY OF   77
               NONVERBAL LANGAUGE INTEGRATION

Chapter Thirteen: GENERAL GUIDELINES FOR USING   81
                 NONVERBAL LANGUAGE EXERCISES

Chapter Fourteen: NONVERBAL LANGUAGE EXERCISES FOR   85
                 INNERVATING THE VENTRAL VAGUS NERVE

Chapter Fifteen: CASE EXAMPLES   95

Chapter Sixteen: CONSIDERATIONS FOR FUTURE EXPLORATION   105

Chapter Seventeen: PEER REVIEW   109

EPILOGUE   113

REFERENCES CITED   119

THE AUTHOR   131

INDEX   133

PREFACE

My goal in creating this guidebook is to offer you a new way of thinking about and managing the autonomic nervous system. The theory of Nonverbal Language Integration shows how the ventral vagus nerve pathway of rapport can be exercised consciously and toned directly through specific facial expressions, gestures, and postures. "When the individual is in the unit of treatment, it is customary to seek a level of rapport with each client" (Andrews and Andrews, 2000:25). Rapport involves "a close or sympathetic relationship: agreement; harmony" (Webster's Dictionary, 2018). "Rapport consists of respect and trust between clinician and client, a feeling of confidence in the clinician by the client, and understanding by both" (King and Berger, 1971:5). This guidebook is intended for those practitioners in healthcare related fields who desire to *use* and *teach* nonverbal language behaviors as tools that exercise the vagus nerve pathways important for rapport. The goal is to establish positive relationships for optimum interpersonal communication (see page 32) in order to gain trust and cooperation. This guidebook is for you if establishing, maintaining, and improving rapport with others are important aspects of your services.

The word "tool" is emphasized in this guidebook rather than "treatment" because nonverbal language behaviors (pragmatics) are important elements of interpersonal communication and essential for successful rapport. While semantics and syntax are about the words and how they are combined, pragmatics involves the behaviors of the body from postures to finely tuned vocalizations. The feelings and intentions behind the words are expressed through pragmatics. This guidebook validates that pragmatics is more than a tool for expressing one's moods and intentions to others. Chapter by chapter, it builds the theory of how pragmatics 1) influences the way our autonomic nervous system perceives and communicates threats and 2) reestablishes a sense of security through vagus nerve activation when it is deemed safe to be at ease and interact positively with others.

The theory of Nonverbal Language Integration argues that the client, family/caregiver, and clinician can enhance rapport voluntarily through specific nonverbal language behaviors. Chapter Twelve explains this theory. Speech-language pathologist Audrey Holland, Ph.D., (2007:3, 38) identifies optimism and reliance to be essential factors in counseling and that they are teachable skills. Holland stresses the importance of focusing on what is right with an individual rather than what is wrong. In this guidebook, you will discover how nonverbal language behaviors can continue to be "right" with an individual and are "teachable" even when communication is significantly impaired. Chapter Thirteen and Chapter

Fourteen are dedicated to toning vagus nerve pathways for rapport through specific nonverbal language behavior exercises. Prior to these chapters, I invite you to join me on the journey of exploration and discovery that led to this theory.

Chapter by chapter, research-based findings are interwoven with the story of how I developed the theory of Nonverbal Language Integration and identified the natural behaviors that activate the vagus nerve pathways. The theory evolved from integrating three important areas of research for evidence-based practice. This involved an objective in-depth review of the research literature regarding neurophysiology, including the Polyvagal Theory by psychologist Stephen Porges, Ph.D. Chapter Seven, "The Ventral Vagus Nerve and Rapport," explores the Polyvagal Theory as related to interpersonal communication and rapport.

Chapter One shares the news story about how a compression collar for preventing concussions in sports does the same thing as the "mysterious" yawn. Knowing that the yawn enhanced engagement inspired me to do informal experimentation on myself and then on others in real-life settings (ethology). My observations triggered questions, the answers inspired dedicated informal research, and my discoveries motivated me to explore the applications of Nonverbal Language Integration to my profession. Ultimately, I observed its influence on establishing rapport with communicatively impaired adults who were hospitalized. Chapter Fifteen, "Case Examples," shares these patients' subjective reporting regarding the theory and the impact of the exercises on their sense of wellbeing. It includes my clinical observations of their participation and how the exercises benefitted me as the clinician.

In many ways, the theory of Nonverbal Language Integration has been long in the making. It evolved from my knowledge and skills accumulated as a healthcare speech-language pathologist since 1976, and from a small private practice that focused on teaching the importance of pragmatics for effective speaking to employees in corporations during the 1990s. Yet, its inspiration was not sparked until July 2018 after reading about the invention of a compression collar that prevents concussion in sports and its similarity in function to the yawn and sucking though a straw. I began my explorations and literature research after experiencing how similar tactile pressure on the neck improved my mood even though I was not aware of any stress.

The first five chapters share my informal experiments and literature research, which were done solely for personal reasons. I did not have any intention of writing a guidebook for clinical practitioners. My initial intent was to help myself pass my blood pressure test at a medical office and then to help my three grandchildren calm their boisterous arguments. However, I have enjoyed doing research and writing for decades. I have published three books for the general public as well as created unpublished workbooks for doing training.

My grandchildren know that I have written books, and they are the ones who insisted that I write about what I was teaching them. Friends and family also encouraged me to document my findings because they had difficulty understanding why I was so excited about experimenting with collars and pressing on necks. Sharing the information meant that I needed to develop a clear hypothesis regarding what was happening and then research neurophysiology in order to try to disprove it. One hypothesis led to another until a theory was born. By Chapter Six, "The Cranial Nerves of Social Engagement," I realized that the findings could be very applicable to my practice as a speech-language pathologist as well to other clinical fields. Each hypothesis is in italics.

In May 2019, I shared the development of the theory of Nonverbal Language Integration and a few exercises during an informal in-service for the rehabilitation staff at a hospital for adults with respiratory failure. I have been the on-call speech-language pathologist there since 2002. The focus of the in-service was on activating the vagus nerve pathways to reduce stress. Initially, the participants were skeptical about how a collar that prevents concussion ultimately inspired a theory about specific nonverbal language behaviors activating the vagus nerve in ways that generates a greater sense of ease. I invited them to complete a pre- and post-training questionnaire about their confidence in calming themselves and their patients quickly, motivating a patient who refused treatment to participate more quickly, and teaching others about the theory. The response was that confidence went from being average to highly confident. This was an additional factor for evidence-based practice—the perceptions of the patient-care staff.

In May 2019, I also had my annual physical. I passed my blood pressure test in a medical office for the first time in years. My physician was surprised when I shared that I had been exercising my vagus nerve naturally and what the specific nonverbal language behaviors are. He requested a copy of the unpublished manuscript. That made me realize that the theory needed to go through a peer review process. The formal reviewer of the guidebook was a speech-language pathologist. The process of the review and results are in Chapter Seventeen: "Peer Review."

As I mentioned, my goal for creating this guidebook is to offer a new theory about how you can use nonverbal language behaviors and the cranial nerves to balance the autonomic nervous system. Step-by-step, you will discover their innate interrelationships, which activates the vagus nerve pathways to return the body to homeostasis and establish rapport. In this way, clients can experience their own ability to generate a greater sense of wellbeing fairly quickly without necessarily engaging in the mental activities of reflection, thinking critically, and reframing. Instead, the autonomic nervous system is rebalanced voluntarily through specific nonverbal language behaviors. This resets the physiology of rapport in order for clients to be prepared to participate in evidence-based activities based on treatment goals. This is an important reason for establishing rapport. Chapter Seven, "The Ventral Vagus Nerve and Rapport," discusses this in depth.

I continue to observe how children and adults experience a greater sense of wellbeing within difficult situations when they activate the vagus nerve pathways directly through the innate tools of specific nonverbal language behaviors. When clients, families, and caregivers discover that they can reduce their stress and the stress of others through their own natural system of regulating emotional responses, resilience and optimism is experienced. The Epilogue discusses these behaviors as ethnology's innate releasing mechanisms (or IRMs). This discussion identifies another reviewer of the guidebook—a Jungian analyst.

Rebalancing the autonomic nervous system for establishing interpersonal communication and rapport is an innate mode of functioning. This means it is what people do already. The theory of Nonverbal Language Integration merely brings a voluntary element to what is already happening phylogenetically. Therefore, the theory and exercises are appropriate to use with individuals across the lifespan, from infants to the elderly. The cover photo demonstrates how I was engaging in one natural behavior with my infant grandson seven years ago.

Chapter Sixteen, "Considerations for Future Exploration," calls for more research. More research is needed to understand the neurophysiology behind this theory in even greater detail. Research is needed to determine the clinical populations that can benefit from this theory, the exercises, and its effects on outcomes. It calls upon you to think about how the theory of Nonverbal Language Integration and exercises can be explored further and applied within your scope of practice. My contact information is in The Author if you would like to share your thoughts and ideas with me.

ONE

A SPORTS COLLAR DOES WHAT?!

"A discovery is said to be an accident meeting a prepared mind."
Albert Imre Szent-Gyorgi (Rosenberg, 2017:xxv)

In July 2018, my husband, Chuck, and I were on vacation in South Lake Tahoe, Nevada. We had just walked to a restaurant and were sitting across from each other eating lunch. I asked a question in order to share a thought. "Imagine a construction worker helping to build a movie theater. He fell off the roof and suffered a head injury. What would you think about the industry?" Chuck replied that he hoped the person recovered and that he would still enjoy going out to see a movie.

"Yes," I agreed. "So, I want to let you know that I have forgiven football." Chuck raised his eyebrows in surprise and then frowned skeptically. I explained that this question came to me on the way to the restaurant when I saw construction workers on a roof. The question was followed by my sudden realization that football players and construction workers who build movie theaters both work in the area of entertainment. They are comparable to actors who risk injury while doing stunts.

Being a speech-language pathologist (SLP) in healthcare since 1976, I have worked with many individuals who have suffered head injuries. A large percentage of rehabilitation professionals do not respect football because of the injuries, including concussions to more severe head injuries. Plus, research now shows that a significant number of "retired" football players acquire dementia. Chuck, who loves football, knows my scorn towards the sport and how I have equated it to the ancient times when spectators watched the gladiators.

I explained my change in attitude and my willingness to view football as another form of entertainment where workers are paid for taking physical risks. Chuck's response surprised me. He said that he had recently seen a program about what we can learn from animals. It included a segment about a "Q Collar" that is reducing concussions. I asked him why he had not told me about it earlier. He said it never occurred to him. I suspected he did not tell me because I had not respected the sport. After lunch, he went off to a casino; I went to our room to do an Internet search of the Q Collar. This was not unusual because we had been coming to South

Lake Tahoe twice a year since 2000. While Chuck enjoys playing craps, I always find Lake Tahoe to be an exceptionally inspiring place to do research and write.

The first paragraph in the first article that I read immediately caught my interest. "The most promising research into concussion prevention is inspired by human yawns, woodpecker tongues, and mountain-dwelling rams. The manifestation of this work is the novel Q Collar, a device worn around the neck that works by enhancing the brain's own physiology. Lightly compressing the jugular vein increases blood volume to the skull. That may help the brain from moving around in the skull, which could reduce traumatic brain injury" (Lemire, 2017). The word "yawns" is what captured my attention. I had no idea at this time that exploring the Q Collar would open up endless avenues for discovery through literature research, informal experimentation, and objective observations within a relatively unexplored interrelationship: neck compression, omohyoid muscles, and the yawn.

The inspiration for the Q Collar came from internist David Smith, M.D. While he was giving a lecture, someone suggested that science needed to determine why the woodpecker can bang its head against a tree and not suffer a head injury. Dr. Smith began researching biomimicry with the specific interest of studying animals within nature for clues to solving the human problem of concussion. His initial focus was on woodpeckers and then head-ramming sheep. Both are unharmed by the massive blows to the head. It was the "crazy tongue" of the woodpecker that inspired Smith to investigate the purpose of the omohyoid muscle, which is in all animals with vertebrates. "When the muscle actually activates, it literally pulls straight back and collapses your jugular. This happens each and every time you yawn" (Lemire, 2017). Dr. Smith said it is the same mechanism used when sucking through a straw or turning the head side to side.

Smith then investigated the big horn sheep, which live in higher elevations. Since there is less oxygen at higher altitudes, their bodies compensate by sending more blood flow to the brain. A video linked to this article explained it further. Slight jugular vein compression produces a "minor and natural" effect of diverting a small portion of blood from the jugular vein to the vertebral arteries in the neck. This causes them to dilate slightly and increase blood volume to the brain. The Q Collar's gentle pressure on the jugular vein slows blood flow out of the brain. Meanwhile, the carotid artery continues sending blood to the brain, which creates an "artificial air bag" between the brain and the skull. The Q Collar is similar to wearing a necktie.

White matter is the "axon super highways" for brain-body connections. Research has shown no change in the brain's white matter in those players who wore the Q Collar. However, evidence of harmful changes is seen in the brains of those who did not wear the collar. In regard to football, one researcher in the video said, "If we can make this game better and make it safe, why wouldn't we want to do that?"

Bauer Neuro Shield is the company that was working on governmental approval of the concussion collar, and they called it the Neuro Shield. Their video overview is in the same link (Lemire, 2017). Their studies took place at a "state-of-the-art" sports center at Cincinnati Children's Hospital. The stated purpose was to determine if the collar, which is worn directly against the neck, preserves the structure of the brain. No one is excluded from using it, and there are sizes for younger kids to adults. However, the subjects were athletes engaging in contact sports.

The Neuro Shield simply puts light pressure on the sides of the neck, so it is a comfortable device. Yet, there is a noticeable difference in the preserved structure of the brain for those who wore it while playing football verses those who did not. According to the researchers, the Neuro Shield uses our own physiology similar to when we *yawn*, *sneeze*, *grunt*, or *lie down*. The collar is not doing something abnormal to the body but imitates something that it already does. An excitement continued to build within me because both the yawn and grunt are often stimulated as part of voice therapy exercises in speech therapy.

In the video, Greg Myer, Ph.D., stated that nature has had millions of years to perfect what is happening – preventing "slosh." Brain slosh is the concept of the brain moving inside the skull. The more energy that the brain absorbs upon impact, the more damage is caused. Closed containers that are only partially filled with fluid absorb and exert more energy. When a container is fully filled, the energy cannot get in and therefore cannot be absorbed. The Neuro Shield is preventing slosh. Slosh is not something we address as SLPs, but the omohyoid muscle is.

In the video, Myer stated that the "omohyoid is only used when we yawn." Yet, it was stated in the article and in the video that these researchers viewed the purpose of the yawn to be a mystery. Being an SLP, and therefore highly trained in the function of the larynx and the treatment of voice and swallow problems, I knew that the omohyoid has many more uses. At the very minimum, the omohyoid is important for voicing certain nonverbal sounds, the articulation of low vowels, and the swallow. Also, neuroscience has shown that the yawn promotes engagement.

What was new for me is that the omohyoid muscle is also involved in preventing concussion. As I just mentioned, the researchers had commented that the Neuro Shield uses the same physiology that happens when we grunt or sneeze, or lay down. Suddenly, pieces of this sports story—*collar, jugular vein compression, omohyoid muscles, grunt, sneeze,* and *the yawn*—became clues to some mystery of interrelationship. I had become hooked. Little did I know at the time that my "accidental" discovery of the invention of the Q collar would not just open up pathways to endless research of the literature; it would change my life. I could not stop asking myself, "What do all these factors have in common in regard to function?" What do you think might be the common denominator?

Two

LOOKING FOR CLUES

"Where knowledge is lacking a clue will appear at the right time."
Eppinger and Hess (1915:2)

In the summer of 2018, I did not realize that my search to discover what jugular vein compression, omohyoid muscles, grunting, sneezing, and the yawn had in common would result in my ability to improve my mood and concentration. Even more, I had no idea that I would develop my observations into a working hypothesis and, ultimately, into a theory. My initial goal was to learn more about the jugular compression collar. The first research article that I read was about the actual studies being done at Cincinnati Children's Hospital Medical Center, which has a sports laboratory (DiCesare et al., 2017). The researchers used a fabric band as a compression collar to evaluate if there were any negative effects from light jugular vein compression.

The study's focus was to determine if compression of the jugular vein and the accumulation of blood in the "compensatory reserve volume" (area between the brain and the skull) might prevent athletes from performing at their highest level. DiCesare et al. evaluated how well eighteen healthy adults over the age of eighteen tolerated the collar during competitive sports-related exertion. The research took place in a "state-of-the-art human performance laboratory" at The SPORT Center and Human Performance Laboratory, Division of Sports Medicine, Cincinnati Children's Hospital Medical Center. Changes in biochemistry, strength, power, and posture were monitored in order to determine if there were any detrimental actions that could adversely affect an athlete's performance goals and abilities.

The results showed that modification of blood flow did not negatively affect an athlete's performance. "The physical and neuromuscular capabilities that were measured in this study were unchanged as a result of wearing the collar" (DiCesare et al., 2017:e28). Nothing was mentioned about there being any improvements in performance. However, the researchers postulated that from "an evolutionary standpoint, it would be reasonable to conclude that phenotypic presence of the omohyoid and digastric compression of the jugular vein would not be selected if their presence had a deleterious effect on survival" (DiCesare et al., 2017:e28).

The research on the compression collar at Cincinnati Children's Hospital showed no negative changes in the biomechanics of performing sports-related tasks. Yet, I recalled that marine biologist and reporter Danni Washington in the *Xploration* program about the compression collar (Washington, n.d.) acknowledged getting a better score on a gross motor skill task that tested mental ability while wearing the Neuro Shield. DiCesare et al.'s study demonstrated that the collar produces no adverse affects and is safe to use. It was stated again that the collar is merely mimicking what animals already use: the omohyoid and the yawn. I knew about both.

What I had put together so far is that a novel collar has been invented that produces jugular vein compression. The only theory that sports medicine has been investigating is whether the collar lowers the risk of concussion in contact sports. Yet, I hypothesized there is much more that this collar does. That is, at the very least, because of the yawn. The yawn has persisted in human evolution despite cultural discouragement. I already knew that the yawn was very misunderstood and had de-evolved in status culturally. It is considered to be a sign of disrespect in many cultures. It has become assumed that the yawn has no use other than to signify fatigue and boredom, and most students learned early to stifle it in the classroom. Some researchers claim that the contagious yawn is a form of empathy, while others disagree and continue to ponder the yawns purpose. However, several years ago, I read that neuroscientists had recently discovered the opposite.

According to authors Andrew Newberg, M.D. and Mark Waldman in *How God Changes the Brain* (2010), brain research based on MRI (magnetic resonance imaging) studies has shown that the yawn's purpose is to heighten focus and attention. However, I did not have this book with me when I began doing the initial research at South Lake Tahoe. I did not recall the specifics of how the yawn was produced or its various functions. Besides, current research for the Neuro Shield had obtained scientific data regarding its function. The yawn puts pressure on the jugular vein due to innervation of the omohyoid muscle, which brings the tongue back and lowers the larynx. I knew from voice and swallowing therapy that the yawn is a function of the omohyoid muscle. I did recall that Newberg and Waldman wrote that neuroscience shows that the yawn innervates the attention centers in the brain. I did not return to Newberg and Waldman's book until after engaging in early informal observations and developing a hypothesis while on that one-week vacation. Details on the neurophysiology of the yawn are in Chapter Seven: The Complexity of the Yawn.

I combined the information I had acquired so far into a testable hypothesis. *If the compression collar creates a similar physiological reaction as the yawn, and the yawn has the ability to heighten focus and attention, then tactile pressure on the sides of the neck in the same location of the collar would trigger a positive shift in attention and focus. I began testing this out on my own neck.* My efforts included observing my responses and searching for research that would disprove the hypothesis. It was important to me that the process remained within the scope of practice of speech-language pathologists (SLP), so I reviewed the American Speech-Language-Hearing Association's (ASHA) guidelines.

According to ASHA, SLPs are engaged in professional practices in the areas of communication and swallowing across the lifespan. Communication and swallowing are broad terms encompassing many facets of function. Communication includes speech production and fluency, language, voice, resonance, body language, and hearing. Swallowing involves many motor and sensory functions from the eyes to the diaphragm, including related feeding behaviors. SLPs are autonomous professionals who are the primary care providers of speech-language pathology services (ASHA Scope of Practice, 2016).

SLPS are trained in the tactile stimulation of the face and neck as part of speech, voice, and swallowing therapy. However, I could not find any research studies that were investigating correlations between touching the neck and attention. I began with the one readily available subject whose neck I could experiment on constantly: myself. Also, besides being an SLP, my personal journey through family losses in 2000 and 2001 inspired me to pursue a doctorate in ministry with emphasis on understanding the role feelings and emotions play in building resilience after any loss. I had become an astute observer of my own body sensations from experience and training.

I began by putting light tactile pressure on both sides of my larynx just above the collarbone without any objective in mind except to focus on any shift in sensations. In speech therapy, ten seconds is often a sufficient amount of time for tactile stimulation to cause a shift in awareness, which is demonstrated by a behavioral change (even if just eye gaze). Also, a yawn often lasts about ten seconds. I pressed for ten seconds and then let go. I immediately noticed a positive shift in my mood, which remained after I let go. Even though I had no awareness of any stress, I actually felt better and, surprisingly, more uplifted. I did it again after waiting one minute. The positive sensation returned before I let go. The positive mood was triggered each time I did it. There were no negative sensations or lowered mood during this subjective experimentation. What do you notice when you do it?

The sensations definitely sparked my interest, partly because of my additional credentials. In 2006, I received my doctorate of ministry from Wisdom University in

San Francisco, CA, with emphasis on honoring feelings and resolving loss. Simultaneously, while working on this degree, I attended the Chaplaincy Institute for Interfaith Ministries in Berkeley, CA. I was ordained the same year. While these new credentials were part of my own healing process from the loss of our fourteen-year old daughter in 2000, I discovered they significantly added to my skill set as an SLP. My dissertation included a workbook for identifying feelings as physiological sensations (such as light, airy, tight, constricted) and emotions as perceptions (such as angry, mad, embarrassed, happy, etc.). It included a writing format (journaling) for integrating feelings and emotions with a cognitive process for enhancing problem solving that transformed awareness regarding any loss (Bohntinsky, 2017). So, I considered myself to be adept at recognizing and abiding with sensations that arose and using critical thinking skills to transform them into opportunities for making changes.

However, I had a physiological problem that I was unable to resolve. Even though my blood pressure is normal, it is abnormally high when taken at a medical office. In May 2018, my physician suggested that I consider taking a low dose of blood pressure medication. This did not make sense to me, because it was normal, even when taken while I was working at a hospital. I believed I have what is called "white coat anxiety." I experience a heightened level of anxiety when I am the patient. This suggests that I have a form of reactive high blood pressure (common among healthcare workers when they are patients), which meant that I had both normal and high blood pressure. I realized that relaxation strategies and cognitive reframing were not helping. In fact, they made it worse when I waited for my blood pressure to be taken the second time. I had been pondering this dilemma because I did not want to take medication for high blood pressure.

Therefore, my sudden shift into a more positive mood when I put light pressure on both sides of my neck was more than just a new experience; it was something that might possibly resolve my blood pressure dilemma. I am certified through Career Advancement and Improvement Opportunities (CIAO, n.d.) to provide VitalStim Therapy to the face and neck. VitalStim Therapy involves "the use of neuromuscular electrical stimulation as part of the therapeutic interventions used in dysphagia." However, I had never read that putting light pressure on the sides of the neck could trigger a positive shift in mood. Yet, I felt uplifted each time I pressed on my neck in the similar location as the compression collar. I was not engaging in any mental activities to improve my mood because I was on vacation. There were no immediate concerns. The only objective that I had in mind was to see what happened in regard to sensations. My consistent observation was that I felt better each time I touched the sides of my neck even though I had not felt negative.

This brought to mind another area of practice in speech-language pathology, which inspired me even more. Nonverbal language (the body language of postures, gestures, and facial expressions) plays a significant role in communication. I was aware of research demonstrating that voluntary body postures and facial expressions elicit different moods. I knew that holding a pencil between the teeth elicits a more positive mood than when the lips were pulled down. A "Superman" pose elicits a mood of strength while slumped shoulders triggers a sense of defeat. Then I recalled the universal gesture of consolation: an adult (especially male) standing behind an upset child (often his son) and placing his hands on the neck and shoulders of the child. Later, I asked two men who had sons if they had ever done this to console their child who was upset, and they said, "yes."

I realized that gently reaching for one's own throat is a natural gesture that often accompanies experiences that are perturbing and, possibly, even indirectly life threatening. It may be accompanied by a "gasp" created by inhalation, which is followed by a longer exhalation (a sigh) or quick exhalation (a grunt). The grunt has been identified as a function of the omohyoid muscles. The throat-grasping gesture (with the thumb on one side and the fingers on the other) presses on the sides of neck similar to the collar. The gasp is produced by innervation of the omohyoid muscle (plus other muscles), and includes the lowering the larynx in the manner of the yawn and final stage of the swallow. I yawned voluntarily and compared sensations. I swallowed paying close attention to each stage. My fingers felt similar contractions on the outside of my neck (palpation), and I could feel similar sensations of tension within my throat.

These observations and experiences combined with my professional knowledge provided enough reliable evidence to make it worthwhile to do more research. Yet, there was nothing more that I could find about the Q Collar or Neuro Shield, and the product was not available in the United States due to undergoing FDA approval. Plus, it was only being evaluated in the field of sports for the purpose of retaining the structure of the brain after the head being struck. I could not find any investigations regarding the compression collar and focus. Also, I did not know the physiology of how the omohyoid muscle (which lowers the larynx) and jugular vein were involved in creating a positive mood. I suspected that some slight increase of blood flow to the cerebral cortex was enhancing focus and attention.

I turned to searching the research literature through ASHA. I found one study that was remotely related. The results were that intrinsic laryngeal musculature activity occurred at abnormally high levels in certain women with normal voice function who were subjected to a stressful speech preparation task. These muscles (the posterior cricoarytenoid, posterior cricoarytenoid, thyroarytenoid/lateral cricoarytenoid muscle complex, and cricothyroid) significantly increased in activity during a non-vocal stress test (Helou, et al., 2018).

This study caused me to wonder if I was like these women. Do I experience some kind of increased intrinsic muscle activity even though I do not consciously perceive a situation as stressful? However, I had already observed repeatedly that my mood elevated when I pressed on my neck. And I knew that positive moods enhance the ability to pay attention and think positively. It made sense that the yawn, and, therefore, the omohyoid, may actually trigger a shift in our physiological state. I suspected that these intrinsic muscle movements within the larynx were also triggering an improved sense of mood during a stressful activity.

Since the compression collar produces similar physiological reactions as the yawn, then there is something the collar, yawn, sucking, grunting, and omohyoid muscles all have in common. Yet, did the pressure on the sides of the neck only stimulate a more positive mood on the population of individuals who had intrinsic muscle activity during stressful situations? Or, did it stimulate a positive mood in others as well? What do you think?

I recalled that the research on the yawn showed that it heightened focus and attention in general. It was time to do more research on myself. What would be your next step?

Three

FROM INFORMAL EXPLORATION TO A HYPOTHESIS

"Truth in science can best be defined as the working hypothesis best suited to open the way to the next better one."   Konrad Lorenz Zacharias

It was time to test more than putting hand pressure on my neck. I needed to make a collar that put consistent pressure on my neck in order to observe what happens in different situations with both of my hands free. Also, I wanted to avoid the sensation of my fingers on my throat because that was an added variable. I was still on vacation so I went to the local drug store in South Lake Tahoe to search for supplies. I settled on a firm headband, neon-green tennis ball plugs for walkers, and a bag of rubber bands. My intent for the collar was different from the Q Collar's or Neuro Shield's purpose of preserving the integrity of the brain. I wanted to observe the effects of neck compression on my mood and my ability to concentrate while engaged in activities. I devised a "collar" that put that same light pressure on the sides of my neck in order to compresses the jugular vein. It became my Jugular Collar—J Collar for short. My first experiment was to wear it while engaged in academic reading and studying the research literature. While my observations were subjective, I sensed that I was reading complex material for longer periods with less need to pause, stand up, or walk around.

The longest test of the J Collar was the four-hour car ride home to the Bay Area. Chuck does most, if not all, the driving. Generally, I would throw my hands forward whenever we got too close to the car ahead of us. This did not happen on the drive home even though heavy traffic occurred in a few places. By the time I arrived home, I felt something very positive had happened on a subtle level of sensations. Yet, I was only the passenger. My focus while driving had not been a component being assessed. I began wearing the J Collar while driving, and there were no negative sensations or emotions. Instead, I actually felt a greater sense of ease on the freeway and in traffic. Then I wore it while transporting our three young grandchildren in the back seat. I realized that I remained calmer when they became boisterous.

Next came the opportunity to experiment with a few willing others: my three grandchildren. In the summer of 2018, our granddaughter was eight years old, and our two grandsons were ages six and four. The first experiment simply involved gently pressing on the sides of their necks. I did this with each grandchild on a separate occasion without giving any information about what I was doing. I pressed for a count of ten and then let go. "How do you feel?" I asked. Each one gave a positive reply, usually, "Good." Yet, they may simply have been humoring their Grams.

An opportunity arose to test the effects of neck compression further. Our youngest grandson loves to pretend that he is a statue and for me to "transport" him on a hand truck (dolly). One day while all three grandchildren were visiting, he asked to ride on the dolly. After watching his brother, our other grandson (who gets nauseous on carnival rides) asked for a turn. However, he quickly became anxious as he watched the ground move beneath him. After about five seconds, he pleaded to get off. I asked him if I could press on the sides of his neck. I pressed for a count of ten and then invited him to get back onto the dolly. "Wow, this is fun!" he exclaimed, and he rode on it for several trips up and down the driveway.

Our granddaughter came outside to see what everyone was doing. I asked her if she wanted to ride on the dolly. She got on and held onto the bars. However, as soon as I lowered it and began moving her around, she too became nervous as the ground passed by below her. "Please stop," she said in a shaky voice. I asked her if I could press on her neck. I pressed for a count of ten and then invited her to get back on. She also exclaimed how fun it was and asked for more trips after I had taken her up and down the driveway several times. Then all three of my grandchildren began arguing for turns and pulling on the dolly, so I put it away. Yet, I knew something had happened that immediately enabled the two grandchildren to override sensations of fear. The pressure on their necks may have helped them to break through protective survival reactions when a real threat did not exist.

My next experiment with the J Collar was to use it during strenuous manual labor. I had spent a day tiling the two floors of our small barn, which I was converting to an art studio. The first day required extensive squatting in order to measure for tile cuts, put down the adhesive mortar, place the large tiles, and wipe them off. I will confess that, not only was there a lot of grunting, swearing occurred multiple times during the process. It had not occurred to me to wear my J Collar, but I did wear it the following day while tiling the second room. Even though I was sore from so much squatting the day before, I noticed that I did not grunt as much. Plus, I did not swear at all even though the floor areas had become more complicated to tile, such as around doorways. I observed that I measured the floor, measured and cut tiles, applied the mortar, squatted down, set in the tiles, and washed them off with greater physical and mental ease.

I realized that I had observed an improvement in performance doing a much more difficult task than Danni Washington's in the *Xploration*. This experience motivated me to become a wearer of the J Collar as well as a "researcher," and I made myself another one. That way, I kept one in the car for driving and one in the house as needed. I did not wear it in public due to its odd look—a bit like old fashion headphones with a black band and neon green earphones worn around the neck.

It was now time to share some of my observations with a few family members and friends. They allowed me to press on their necks, and everyone's responses were positive. Yet, they may have been humoring me because subtle body language often showed some skepticism. Since beginning the work on my doctorate in the early 2000's and then writing my dissertation, family and close friends had become accustomed to my enthusiasm when it came to exploring ways to transform negative experiences into opportunities for enhancing emotional awareness and critical thinking. Several individuals encouraged me to write when I suggested that I needed to consolidate my notes into an informal document. They were interested in reading the information because they could not quite understand what I was exploring.

I began by reviewing the original source of information behind the Q Collar— animal research. I was aware of the use of animals in research in speech and hearing so I checked to see if animal research had been published through the American Speech-Language-Hearing Association (ASHA) regarding jugular vein compression or the omohyoid muscle. While I could not find anything, I was reminded about the effects of "enriched" verses "impoverished" environments on learning, memory, and problem solving skills (Ansell, 1991). Rats housed with objects that could be manipulated and explored had increased thickness of the cerebral cortex and hippocampus and demonstrated higher functioning. Research like this lead to the development of more creative and enriching treatment programs for individuals with head injuries in the 1990's. I was Director of the Department of Speech Pathology and Audiology at Alameda County Medical Center at the time (1980-2002), and we revised our head injury program as well.

Animal research has been done on mice to better understand the anatomy of the human voice (Thomas, et al., 2009). The omohyoid muscles were not addressed. I could not find anything regarding exploring biomimicry (looking to nature to create sustainable solutions) or ethology (the study of animals in their natural settings) in the field of speech language pathology. According to Wikipedia, ethology is the scientific exploration of animal behavior in natural settings because of the basic premise that behaviors are evolutionary adaptive traits. One of the founders of modern ethology is Austrian zoologist Konrad Zacharias Lorenz, who shared the 1973 Nobel Prize in Physiology or Medicine. He is known for his investigations of imprinting as an instinctive bond. I knew that the importance of human infant bonding had become well recognized. More importantly, I realized that I had been engaged in a form of ethology by studying my grandchildren and myself in natural settings.

I began to hypothesize that light jugular vein compression from a collar or by the fingertips was causing a positive shift in mood. At that time, my goal was simply to help my grandchildren manage their conflicts and fears, help myself with my blood pressure tests, and find research that either validated or disproved my hypothesis. If validated, I would share something in writing with a few friends.

I had no idea that I would develop, discard, build upon evolving hypotheses, and, ultimately, combine my findings into a theory. I had not even entertained the possibility of offering the information to other clinicians. Yet, from what I have shared with you so far, could jugular vein compression be activating some evolutionary trait that enriches us from within? If so, what might that "adaptive trait" be?

Four

HOW DOES JUGULAR VEIN COMPRESSION IMPROVE MOOD AND FOCUS?

The oral, laryngeal, and pharyngeal cavities together are among the most diverse and rich sensory systems of the body.   Ianessa Humbert (2011:10).

My subjective observations of my grandchildren's and my own positive responses to neck compression motivated me to take the next step in my research. I decided that the next phase involved inviting others to participate in these explorations. This meant that I needed to compile my notes regarding the data and observations about jugular vein compression into a more formal working document. I also needed to make more J Collars and develop a research plan. *I hypothesized that the added blood flow was also going to the forebrain of the cerebral cortex, which was resulting in improvements similar to enriched environments.* This meant that I had to understand how the change in blood volume from jugular vein compression was affecting the cerebral cortex neurologically. Yet, I quickly discarded that hypothesis and moved away from investigating blood flow.

A fairly recent study (Fisher et al., 2015) regarding the jugular vein and hemodynamics disproved my hypothesis that the added blood flow for preventing "slosh" was also going to the forebrain and enhancing concentration. The researchers created compression collars by using gauze that bulged at the point of the jugular vein. They found that pressure on the jugular vein did increase blood volume to the skull by filling the craniums compensatory reserve volume. However, it did not change the cerebral blood flow within the brain nor affect the response of the brain's blood flow to hypercapnia (excess carbon dioxide in the blood). If the compression on the jugular vein was not increasing blood flow to the cerebral cortex, then what do you think was causing the positive shift in mood and focus when I wore a collar or gently pressed on the sides of my neck with my fingertips?

I decided to look in the direction of neural systems and cognitive function rather than blood flow. In regard to neural systems, a SLP's training is on what happens to communication and/or swallow within diagnoses such as congenital disorders,

15

strokes, head injuries, or disease and how to habilitate or rehabilitate the impairments. The focus has not been on helping individuals to enhance what is already acceptably functional in regard to cognition (such as awareness, attention, and memory), language systems, affective or emotive systems, organizational/ abstraction/reasoning skills, and motor/behavioral skills. Generally, the SLP is not involved when an individual's communication skills, which are revealed though an array of learning systems, are deemed to be within "normal" limits for successful independent living.

Yet, enhanced function is what I was observing in myself when I wore my J Collar. My ability to accomplish challenging mental and/or physical tasks with a more positive mood and greater focus was improving even though I seemed to be highly functional for successful living. Now, I had to know the cause in order to determine if the collar was some kind of placebo. Based on my extensive work with adults with neurogenic communication disorders, I knew that, at the very minimum, a client must demonstrate basic cognitive functions regarding awareness and arousal (even if merely involuntary) in order to have sufficient adaptive functions to benefit from speech, language, swallowing, and/or cognitive therapy. Therefore, I changed my focus to investigating cognition.

Awareness involves accessing information from the environment using one or more of the five senses. I turned my research to hearing because it is a well-documented sense in terms of its development, application, and remediation of deficits. Investigating auditory behaviors resulted in discovering data from 1970 that expanded my thinking regarding my observations from jugular vein compression. Rita Eisenberg (1970:459) explained that signals from the environment cause motor responses or "inaction" depending on needs regarding "flight, feeding, reproduction and the like." According to Eisenberg, the auditory nerve became highly elaborated in "acquisition societies" when survival evolved to depend on successful economics. The processing of "communicative codes" became more crucial than gross muscle strength and agility.

Hearing involves picking up a range of frequencies. According to Eisenberg, low frequencies are effective inhibitors of distress and evoke gross motor responses. High frequencies tend to elicit freezing reactions similar to most animals. Reactions to these frequencies evolve beyond infancy into different attributes, which fall under "affect." The acoustics of musical instruments and alarm signals produce different states within us from distaste and annoyance to pleasure. "In sum, whatever the context in which psychological responses to sound are studied, low frequencies invariably have "good" or "pleasure" connotations, and high frequencies the reverse. . . . Qualitative judgments of sound in adult life—those related to 'noisiness' and the like . . . may have their roots in preadapted mechanisms referable to the phylogenetic past" (Eisenberg, 1970:462-463).

I thought about the human voice and what happens when hearing low to high frequencies within an extreme pitch range. A voice at optimum midrange is soothing while high pitches, such as a scream, can cause wincing. The larynx must be in a low position for lower pitches and also for a yawn, which is followed by a natural midrange laryngeal position and optimum pitch of a relaxed sigh. Cheek and lip muscles relax during the production of lower frequencies. The larynx must rise up and move forward to produce high pitches. There is greater tension in the face and the brows rise when producing high pitches.

I pressed on the sides of my neck. The light pressure made it difficult for me to raise my eyebrows. Producing high pitch sounds seemed like a challenge. I had to use greater conscious awareness to generate enough force to override a sense of resistance. The midrange pitches felt easier to produce. There was no sense of resistance or assistance at my lowest frequency. What happens when you try it?

What about the swallow? The light pressure on my neck did not make it difficult to produce a voluntary swallow, which requires upward movement of the larynx as well. In fact, touching the sides of the neck at the mid level of the larynx is a therapy technique to facilitate the swallow. I knew that the motor (efferent) pathways of the vagus nerve innervate the soft palate, pharynx, larynx, and upper esophagus. Does light pressure on the sides of the neck facilitate the innervation of the vagus nerve for laryngeal lowering and inhibit upward movement? If so, what function might the vagus nerve serve in regard to the heightened sense of positive mood?

Searching for answers led me to look more closely at the swallow after reading how a "continuing" popular theory regarding taste buds continues to be maintained even though it has been disproven (Pelletier, 2002). There is no "tongue map" for flavors. German research in the early 1900's showed sweetness to be on the tip of the tongue and bitter flavors on the back. However, this was disproved in 1974. Even though disproved, the tongue map continued to be published in textbooks. According to Pelletier, it is now known that three cranial nerves are involved with taste buds: the facial, glossopharyngeal, and the vagus nerve. "Taste cells lie within taste buds, which are located in various tongue papillae, hard and soft palate, and root of the tongue. Taste buds also are found in the larynx, but their function is not clearly understood" (Pelletier, 2002:6). Taste is an important function in the trigger of the swallow, yet I had been unaware of the role of the vagus nerve in the sensation of taste.

I looked for more current research regarding the sensory aspects of the swallow. According to Humbert (2011), the importance of the sensory components involved in creating motor movements is becoming highly recognized and is called sensory integration. "The oral, laryngeal, and pharyngeal cavities together are among the most diverse and rich sensory systems of the body" (Humbert, 2011:10). Research has shown that vagus nerve pathways are involved with the muscles in these cavities. Even though the swallow is accomplished within a second, it is not only a reflex in the brainstem but involves "higher brain functions in the cortex" as well. This means awareness is occurring on a cognitive level. The effortless efficiency of the swallow results from a "steady stream of sensory information being processed while planning, executing, and evaluating an action. Sensory input is the information propagated to the central nervous system following stimulation of a group of sensory receptors. Sensory receptors are modality-specific, so sensory nerve endings are receptive to a specific type of sensory information" (Humbert, 2011: 11). One technique to help strengthen an impaired swallow is to vary the flavors.

Tactile is another important sensation for stimulating the swallow. This involves the feel of the utensil on the lips, the food (bolus) on the tongue, teeth, buccal regions, and palate, the movements of the bolus to the back of the throat and into the pharyngeal cavity, the trigger of the swallow, and movement of the bolus into the esophagus. The individual's unconscious assessment of a successful swallow begins with the feedback sensation that the airway is clear and the larynx has returned to its resting state. The next bite begins and the process repeats itself as long as each swallow is successful. Yet, there are more sensory nerve fibers than taste and tactile. In swallowing therapy, the visual presentation of the meal, the eyes scanning the food on the plate, the eye-hand coordination of taking pieces off the plate, and bringing the bite to the mouth are important aspects of the swallow as well. Auditory sensation includes the sounds of chewing and the swallow.

The larynx has been responsible for the swallow long before humans had language; yet, language has expanded the swallow's "role" through metaphor. There are English idioms that use the swallow metaphorically. Ironically, two that came to mind are "A hard pill to swallow" and "Swallow your pride." At this point, I would say that discovering that I was a healthcare worker with "white coat anxiety" was a "tough pill to swallow." Yet, "swallowing my pride" by admitting I may have been righteously indignant about football is what led me to discover the Q Collar. In this research journey, I have been "swallowed up" (to be lost in, to absorb, consolidate, and coalesce) by intriguing data about the vagus nerve. This has led me to be able to "swallow" the possibility that something other than the jugular vein is involved with enhancing mood.

I have observed that putting pressure on the sides of the neck does more than merely facilitate a voluntary dry swallow or the production of optimum pitches. The pressure also creates a more positive mood. What I knew clinically is that impairment of the vagus nerve weakens the musculature essential for a safe swallow, protective cough, and functional voice. Swallowing therapy and voice therapy involve improving these functions through exercises that strengthen and increase the agility of the musculature as well as heighten sensory awareness.

Since I began wearing the collar and then exploring motor behaviors that create similar pressure on the sides of my neck, I have observed significant improvements in my ability to remain calm. I find that I am much more relaxed when my grandchildren become overly boisterous. My ability to engage in complex literature research and writing has improved as well even though I had no goal in mind except to solve this mystery. I now suspected that it is not the compression of the blood flow within the jugular vein that is triggering a positive mood, focused attention, and concentration. It may be that I have been strengthening the sensory (afferent) pathways of the vagus nerve. Just as I did not know that the vagus nerve is involved with taste buds that are on the tongue and within the larynx, I may have missed the "update" *that activation of the vagus nerve through neck compression has a positive affect on mood and focus.* This became my new hypothesis, so I needed to turn to neurophysiology in order to learn more about the vagus nerve pathways.

Five

EXPLORING THE FUNCTIONS OF THE VAGUS NERVE

We can capitalize upon the way the brain normally does this—that is, via learning.
There is overwhelming evidence to indicate that the brain continuously remodels
its neural circuitry in order to encode new experiences and enable behavioral change.
Jeffery Kleim and Theresa Jones (2008:225)

What role does the vagus nerve play in generating the states of calmness and improved focus that I witnessed in my grandchildren and in myself? I used my swallow to check out another hunch through subjective experimentation. I swallowed saliva and checked how long it took to produce another dry swallow. The average time was ten seconds when I did not touch my neck. I had to swipe my tongue inside my mouth repeatedly each time to acquire enough saliva to trigger the swallow. When I pressed lightly on each side of my neck, the voluntary swallow was completed in an average of four seconds. Surprisingly, I did not need to swipe my mouth with my tongue to collect saliva.

I suspected that the light pressure was doing something to stimulate the sensory receptors of the vagus nerve, thus making my dry swallow less effortful. The tactile pressure also made my swallow feel stronger when swallowing liquid or food. I added these observations to my findings that wearing my collar (no longer a jugular collar) made me more productive with less swearing and grunting during physically taxing tasks, and it put me at greater ease while riding in a car or driving a car.

These findings led to my next question. Is there a way to create the same effect without using a collar or generating pressure with the hand? This would require interoception, or the ability to feel one's body states and emotions (Fogel, 2009:39). Press on the sides of your neck and focus on the sensory feedback from the muscles within your throat. Now, palpate your neck for changes in tension and movement regarding the neck muscles. Finally, focus on any movements that occur simultaneously at the tongue base, mouth, cheeks, nose, eyes, and forehead. What catches your attention the most?

I noticed a sensation in my nose. I felt my nostrils widen slightly each time I pressed on the sides of my neck. I then discovered that there was an accompanying increase in visual awareness. It was not a "pinpoint" focus for fine details; it was a more astute focus on the entire visual field. I could not recreate the sensation of enhanced visual attention by widening my eyes or squinting. Yet, when I widened my nostrils voluntarily, this shift in visual awareness accompanied the widening each time. This kind of visual focus is "soft" focus. More importantly, widening my nostrils also produced that similar positive mood.

I began to practice holding the position of widened nostrils, which also results in widening the nares for breathing. It soon became effortless. What facial expression do you think you would see if you looked in a mirror? I believed I would see a very exaggerated expression, so I was surprised to see a serene smile and a relaxed vibrant gaze. I was already aware of research that showed the voluntary smile creating a more positive mood. I had learned decades ago that resting the tongue on the palate produces a silent smile. Since then, I have monitored the position of my tongue as an ongoing practice. Yet now, rather than an exaggerated "posed" facial expression, the mirror reflected an authentic smile and gaze that were inviting even with my tongue lowered. That expression was replaced with furrowed brows when I asked the mirror, "How is this happening?"

Then I got an odd idea to put greater pressure on my neck with my hand. What I saw in the mirror was the universal gesture of grasping one's own neck when extremely startled. My neck "reacted" by producing greater muscle tension. I knew that an impact to the neck could break the larynx, and asphyxiation would result. If the person lives, the swallow would be impaired. Survival would be threatened. This means that if the attack was an attempt to strangle slowly, struggle could compromise the integrity of the larynx and cut off the air supply even more. I suspected that I was experiencing a reflexive tensing of the muscles around the neck, which creates a resistance to the external pressure upon the throat. Interestingly, I did not experience a stressful sense of fight/flight or immobilization reaction. Instead, I noticed my nostrils widened along with the greater tensing of the neck muscles. I thought of a mother feline carrying a kitten by the neck. The skin would naturally tighten around the kitten's neck and produce a relaxation response.

Widening my nostrils created similar, although milder, musculature tightening in my neck. Yet, I experienced that familiar positive mood and sense of heightened awareness. I realized that if neck compression triggered a positive mood and enhanced focus, recall and critical thinking might improve just enough to increase the chances of escaping from a neck hold. The pressure definitely produced a relaxation response within me. If this is a valid observation, then the "reflex" could be a phylogenetically evolved response that promotes survival. I became even more motivated to explore the research literature regarding the roles of the vagus nerve beyond the sensory and motor functions of speech, swallowing, and voice. I discovered much more, including its chemical messenger. What do your think it is?

Gudmundsson (2014) argues his hypothesis regarding an intracranial pressure (ICP) adjustment system and the role of the vagus nerve. He begins by introducing the Monro-Kellie doctrine, which addresses pressure-volume relationships within the skull. This relationship is based on volumes of blood, brain, and cerebral spinal fluid. This doctrine states, "in the fixed intracranial cavity one component can only increase if others are decreased." This helps to maintain homeostasis within the body, and the vagus nerve plays a "major" role (Gudmudsson, 2014: 163).

According to Gudmundsson, the vagus nerve has three pathways: 1) motor, 2) parasympathetic efferents, and 3) sensory afferents. There are sensory fibers (afferents) with nerve endings that originate above the diaphragm in the abdominal and thoracic viscera, from baroreceptors in the aortic and chemoreceptors in the aortic bodies, and all end at the brain stem. They also receive general sensory inputs from the external ear, tympanic membrane, external auditory meatus, larynx, pharynx and esophagus. Over 80% of the fibers of the vagus nerve are afferent viscerosensory fibers (Gudmundsson, 2014:165). The abdominal viscera include the stomach, pancreas, intestine, colon, liver, spleen, kidney, duodenum, adrenal gland, gall bladder, and appendix. The thoracic viscera include the heart, lungs, veins, arteries, trachea, and thyroid gland. Baroreceptors are sensors within blood vessels that relay the information regarding changes in volume and pressure to the cardioinhibitory center of the brainstem. Chemoreceptors are within arteries and are sensitive to oxygen, carbon dioxide, and hydrogen ions levels (Brashers and McCance, 2012:575).

Gudmundsson identifies a secretory function to serve as a "messenger" to the vagus nerve and that the arachnoid granulations produce this messenger. He theorizes that the messenger is nitric oxide (NO). Research has supported the plausibility that there is an intracranial pressure (ICP) adjustment system and an adjusting system that is mediated by the vagal nerve. If the arachnoid granulations produce NO as a response to changes in ICP, the "jugular foramen with the vagus nerve lying just subendothelially is where this message would be received" (Gudmundsson, 2014:167). Of great interest to me was a statement that "neck wrapping reduces cerebral venous outflow from the cranial cavity and thus also reduces CSF [cerebral spinal fluid] elimination, opening up the subarachnoidal space so that the arachnoid granulations can resume their NO production." These findings offered an explanation of how jugular vein compression can trigger the vagus nerve within the jugular foramen. They supported my observation of enhanced mood if nitric oxide is playing a role. Thinking back to the dentist office, nitrous oxide helps me to feel calm and relaxed even though there is fear and, at times, pain. What would you hypothesize at this point?

I realized that the Monro-Kellie doctrine, the jugular vein, vagus nerve, nitric oxide, and neck wrapping could be interconnected in regard to what happens with jugular vein compression from the collar or hand pressure. Nothing I had researched so far suggested that what I observed in terms of positive mood and focused attention are due to some kind of placebo. *I now hypothesized that pressure on or within the neck at the area the jugular vein triggers a reaction that activates the vagus nerve by using nitric oxide as the messenger. This chain of events quickly adjusts the system towards a more positive mode of functioning.*

An adjustment to a state of pleasurable calmness was the best so far that describes what I experienced when I wore my collar, pressed gently on the sides of my neck, or widened my nostrils (which tightens the neck muscles in that location). A search for synonyms of "calm" brought up the word "homeostasis," which means that the body returns to a state of equilibrium. Equilibrium is a state of intellectual or emotional balance, "a state of adjustment between opposing or divergent influences or elements." Another word is "poise." Now, I better understood what I was experiencing. How would you describe what you experience?

But how is the vagus nerve involved with nitric oxide to regulate such homeostasis? I receive nitrous oxide whenever I get my teeth cleaned or have dental work. This enabled me to use nitrous oxide every six months as an opportunity to process feelings around loss that may have been too difficult to do otherwise. I could definitely find similarities in the two experiences: the "adjusted" state I experience with nitrous oxide and the "adjusted" state I experience when I widen my nostrils. Not being a neuroscientist or biochemist, grasping the most technical terms and concepts that I was reading presented a challenge. Yet, there was enough information that I did understand, and these findings inspired me to persevere in researching the literature in these areas.

I had not found anything so far to refute what I was observing. *My hypothesis evolved to postulate that compression on the neck in the area of the jugular vein triggers a physiological reaction that promotes a state of equilibrium without our awareness.* Something is happening at the level of the autonomic nervous system. Searching for information on nitric oxide and the vagus nerve led to the article: "Nitric oxide and hypertension: not just an endothelium derived relaxing factor!" Chowdhary and Townsend (2001:219) wrote:

> *"The autonomic nervous system is another important homeostatic mechanism in the regulation of arterial pressure which also appears to be under the control of nitric oxide. . . . Sympathetic over-activity has been most clearly demonstrated in early hypertension. . . . Impairment of baroreflex mediated vagal responses may also constitute an important permissive factor in the development and maintenance of hypertension. This may be mediated not only by the direct cardio-inhibitory effects of vagal activity but*

also by its ability to block sympathetic signal transduction, the so-called 'indirect vagal' effect.

According to Chowdhary and Townsend, a decrease in nitric oxide is interrelated with the increase in vascular resistance that occurs in individuals with hypertension. Yet, it is possible that it is the hypertension that reduces the nitric oxide. Nitric oxide is generated from L-arginine [amino acid used in the biosynthesis of proteins] by the nitric oxide synthase (NOS). A decrease in the NOS or NO has resulted in increased sympathetic nerve activity and increased renal sympathetic nerve activity, increased blood pressure, and increased heart rate. NO is very likely a "neuromodulator" that limits sympathetic activation during stress by inhibiting the force of muscular contractions ("inotropic responses") to adrenergic stimulation (Chowdhary and Townsend, 2001:222.)

"There is substantial evidence to suggest that NO inhibits cardiac and vascular sympathetic activity both centrally and peripherally. . . . There is good evidence that NO increased activity in brainstem sites promotes efferent vagal activity, and also enhances cardiac response to vagal stimulation." (Chowdhary and Townsend, 2001:221, 223). According to these researchers, studies on ferrets have shown that the vagus nerve not only inhibits cardiac responses but also "exerts a powerful regulatory influence through inhibition of beta-adrenergic responses. . . . Nitric oxide also appears to have a cardiac vagotonic influence in humans." Evidence from research on humans gathered so far is indicating that NO has a significant role "as a neuromodulator of cardiovascular autonomic activity in normal physiology." NO has also been shown to stimulate vagal motor nuclei centrally in the medulla and a central vagotonic effect within the dorsal motor nucleus of the vagus nerve.

Vagotonic refers to vagotonia, which is "hyperirritability of the parasympathetic nervous system" (Thomas, 1973). The Internet dictionary defines vagotonia as "the over activity or irritability of the vagus nerve, adversely affecting function of the blood vessels, stomach, and muscles" (thefreedictionary, n.d.). Vagotonia is not in *Understanding Pathophysiology* by Huether and McCance (2012). Wikipedia added the symptoms of cold hands and feet, cold and clammy perspiration, severe fatigue, and vasovagal syncope. While this information was limited, it could be applicable. But, I needed to continue researching NO. I found one more very important article.

Research shows that NO "has key roles in maintaining homeostasis and in vascular smooth muscle, neurons, and the GI tract. It has a definite role in regulating all aspects of our lives from walking, digestion, sexual functions, pain perception and pleasure, memory recall and sleeping. Finally, the way it continues to function in our bodies will influence how we degenerate with age" (Habib and Ali, 2011:13). Initially discovered as toxic "nitrous air" in 1772, it was not until 1998 that it was identified as a "signaling molecule" important in the protection against disease. The

Noble Prize for Medicine and Physiology was awarded to L. J. Innerro, R. F. Furchgott, and F. Murid for this discovery about NO (Habib and Ali, 2011:1).

I have included complex data throughout this guidebook from my review of the research literature for those who desire to do additional investigations. Personally, I had obtained sufficient data from the literature to realize that I had come full circle in regard to my own "medical problem." I have reactive blood pressure based on the abnormally high readings when taken at a medical office compared the lower normal readings at home. Yet, I had become aware that I was searching out complicated questions and reading highly technical articles on biochemistry without frustration or fatigue. Enjoying doing research like this was not my previous norm.

I found one more article supporting that pressing on the sides of the neck and widening the nostrils stimulate the vagus nerve in some way that enhances a state homeostasis. This includes a more positive mood, heightened attention and focus, and even enhanced outcomes. There is a transcutaneous electrical stimulation device that innervates the vagus nerve in order to relieve psychological disorders such as anxiety, severe depression, and stress.

The device is based on neurological research showing that the autonomic nervous system is extremely complex in regard to anatomy, regulatory systems, and physiological influences. The autonomic nervous system responds to a wide range of stimuli that can stress our systems on physical, emotional, and psychological levels. Neuroimaging studies now show that the vagus nerve "broadly affects different parts of the brain, including the thalamus, cerebellum, orbito-frontal cortex, limbic system, hypothalamus, and medulla" (Conte et. al, 2017: 533). The FDA has approved electrical stimulation of the vagus nerve for treating refractory depression and epilepsy.

There is a new FDA-approved stimulator device, the NuCalm tVNS system, which includes a variety of components. Electrodes are placed on the upper neck at the level of the right and left earlobes to stimulate the sensory auricular branch of the vagus nerve (ABVN). An earlier device was implanted at the level of the cervical branch of the vagus nerve, but it triggered coughing or hoarseness as well as creating other risks. This new NuCalm tVNS system "targets the cutaneous receptive field of the ABVN at the outer ear." The system also includes a cream formulated to produce a relaxation response by "counteracting adrenaline." Binaural noise-dampening headphones are worn to synchronize the brain through "proper frequency bands at the interval (12 Hz – 4Hz.)." Also, the individual wears a "light-blocking eye mask to enhance relaxing brain wave bands such as alpha" (Conte et al., 2017:534). The validity of the device activating the vagus nerve is determined by heart rate variability (HRV).

Heart rate variability (HRV) has been identified as a reliable measure of the autonomic nervous system (ANS), because the heart's rhythm is modulated by the sympathetic and parasympathetic systems within the ANS (Conte et al., 2017:533, 540). The sympathetic system takes control when stressful situations occur "whereas vagal modulation induces normal heart rate dynamics and corrects its intrinsic variability . . . . In healthy humans, heart rate regulation is known to exhibit complex variability over an extensive time dynamic range."

Diminished HRV occurs in nervous system disorders, including some that are psychological. The central point of Conte et al.'s study was that "stimulation of the vagus nerve by a signal that is intrinsically multifractal induces a strong heart related neuro-modulation that enables the subject to recover ANS dysfunction related to his/her psychological disorder" as well as reduce anxiety and stress. The research showed that the NuCalm device produces a multifractal time dynamics output signal (Conte et al., 2017:540). I had no idea what fractal meant, so I researched that term.

Benoit Mandelbrot described fractal geometry within nature in the early 1980's. Now it is being applied to studies in health. There are two main properties of fractals (Franca et al. 2018). First, they consist of parts that are similar to the whole, which is called self-similarity. Secondly, they have a fractional "Hausdorff-Besicovitch" dimension, which is also called fractal dimension. Monofractals are characterized by a single fractal dimension. When an object or system cannot be explained by a single fractal, it becomes multifractal. There are subsets to the system whereby each can be identified by its distinct fractional dimension. Examples of natural phenomena that exhibit multifractal patterns included turbulence in space, soil composition, human physical activity, the heart beat, inter-breath intervals, and even in the dynamics in brain activity. In multifractal systems, the measurements must be accomplished with multifractal tools. "At the very least, additional statistical moments appear to be required to characterize such dynamics. . . . In addition, there are several parameter choices to be made for the purpose of the analysis" (Franca et al. 2018).

The current use of the NuCalm system was important to me, because I am certified in doing electrical stimulation of the musculature for the swallow. I own my own VitalStim device. It was my experience that not one of my patients objected to the "tolerable" level of strong vibrations at their throat. The success of the NuCalm system provided confirmation that stimulation of the vagus nerve promotes an increase sense of wellbeing by placing the body into a more relaxed state. It was acknowledged that physiological stimulation does not usually result in a quick permanent positive change. It takes repetition (which neurostimulation tools could fall under and/or through structured learning strategies) to establish new behaviors. Yet, stimulation of the vagus nerve was actually enabling people with certain psychological disorders to recover. I was also experiencing what I would call a "significant" change as well in regard to more positive behaviors. This fits with what Daniel Goleman and Richard Davidson call "altered traits."

In *Altered Traits* (2017:249, 283), Coleman and Davidson share a saying from Hetsun Milarepa, who is known as an eminent twelfth century Tibetan poet, yogi, and sage. "In the beginning nothing comes, in the middle nothing stays, in the end nothing goes." The authors interpret this as desired habits that evolve with practice. At first skills, especially in contemplation, come and go, but over time "the changes are constant and enduring, with no fluctuation." The authors point out that while learning new traits involves neuroplasticity (experiences "shaping" the brain), "we are typically unaware of these forces." Engaging in mindless pursuits without any specific intentions towards learning results in neurons "dutifully strengthening or weakening the relevant brain circuitry" and this can "lead to haphazard changes in the muscle of the mind."

I realized that while I engaged in contemplation to process life events, something had not carried over to my physiology. Since my blood pressure elevated above normal ranges in the medical office, there may be some over reactivity in general. I now suspected that my blood pressure rose at other times as well because I often experienced a lingering level of anxiety after getting angry. These factors suggest that I have been unaware of "haphazard changes" that "weakened my brain circuitry" and caused me to maintain a stressful level that seemed "normal" to my mind. That is because I noticed immediate shifts to a more positive and relaxed mood whenever I put on the compression collar, pressed on my throat, or widened my nostrils. *If true, then these voluntary behaviors were resulting in more immediate shifts in reducing physiological stress that resides at an unconscious level than those produced by contemplation. Even though I was unaware of feeling stressed, these behaviors triggered a sense of improved homeostasis.*

There was minimal data on the vagus nerve in research published by the American Speech-Language-Hearing Association (ASHA) when I merely searched "vagus nerve." Most of the articles and resources that I have included so far all allow public access. Yet, a December 2018 article, when combined with all my other findings, gave me greater incentive to continue on with my explorations and generate a more formal and cohesive document rather than just trying to pass my blood pressure test at a medical office or sharing the information with friends. Throughout my clinical practice, I had observed that stress occurs in people with communication deficits. Now, ASHA's publications have a current article (Pompon, et al. 2018) that supports my observations, at least for individuals with aphasia.

Communication in itself is "often deemed stressful—described as 'linguistic anxiety'" (Pompon, et al., 2018: 2934). These researchers were looking for ways to measure this stress. While individuals with aphasia reported higher states of depression, frustration, and anxiety than "neurotypical" individuals, they have less "resources" available for coping. Individuals with aphasia have reported having decreased ability to monitor and manage tension. "Prolonged stress not only impacts quality of life and ability to adjust to new life changes but may influence the overall trajectory of recovery."

Stress that only lasts for a couple of months can negatively impact physical, emotional, and cognitive health, and this impacts the ability to learn and remember. Research is now showing that continued stress over time can actually impair the neurological activity that supports attention and memory. "In other words, chronic stress may limit the neuroplastic capacity of the individual and influence his or her ability to learn (Pompon et al. 2018:2935). The researches added, "since chronic stress appears to interfere with an individual's neuroplastic potential, it may therefore limit the success of rehabilitation."

Rehabilitation involves teaching individuals skills to improve function. Recovery involves a natural healing of neural pathways (spontaneous recovery) along with the dynamic plasticity of the neural system that evolves as a result of directed experiences through learning strategies. According to Kleim and Jones (2008:S225), "We can capitalize upon the way the brain normally does this—that is, via learning. There is overwhelming evidence to indicate that the brain continuously remodels its neural circuitry in order to encode new experiences and enable behavioral change. . . . This neuroplasticity is, itself, driven by changes in behavioral, sensory, and cognitive experiences. . . . Learning involves changes in genes, synapses, neurons, and neuronal networks within specific brain regions."

These two articles supported what I was experiencing from the opposite side of the equation. If stress has influence on learning, and ongoing stress can reduce the benefits of learning, then positive mood would enhance the ability to learn and remember. That means positive mood results in better outcomes than when stressed. Learning requires repetition and feedback. I was now becoming assured that I had stimulated my vagus nerve repeatedly for extended periods by wearing the collar and for shorter periods when I widened my nostrils. I had become more relaxed as a passenger in a car and as the driver. I had not found anything so far refuting that the vagus nerve plays a significant role in enhancing positivity.

Something about my learning abilities was changing. Experiencing less stress while engaged in a learning process would offer a simple explanation for how I could now focus longer while reading complex journals and extract salient information with greater ease even when not wearing my collar or voluntarily widening my nostrils. This indicated that my neural circuitry was changing on a level that I was not conscious of. I was aware that I was experiencing a more positive mood when doing such tasks even though I was not directing my efforts towards improving mood or attention. These observations along with the evidence from Pompon et al. (2018) and Klein and Jones (2008) motivated me find a way to bring information about the vagus nerve to my profession and other clinicians. Sharing discoveries regarding improving emotional states was not unusual for me, because I had presented my doctoral work about integrating feelings and emotions with critical thinking at the 2008 ASHA convention in New Orleans.

I am very familiar with a wide range of contemplation techniques, having studied them while pursuing a doctorate of ministry and meeting the interfaith chaplaincy seminary requirements for ordination. My interest was never in the achievement of some form of "enlightened state" of being for its own sake. I was interested in the mindfulness exercises that enhanced awareness of sensations and feelings and enriched critical thinking skills. My goals have been to improve the ability to be resilient when stressful events happen, particularly loss. This is consistent with how Newberg and Waldman (2016:42) describe enlightenment, including how "each step along the way improves the functioning of your brain."

My focus has been on developing conscious awareness of sensations (tight, lose, tingly, firm, etc.) and exploring the effect of emotions (sad, mad, confused, frustrated, etc.) as impressions of perceived states of being in any given situation. Then options for addressing challenging situations expand when using a framework that integrates feelings with critical thinking. This is a framework for contemplation that fits well with the modality of writing (journaling). I published my 2006 dissertation in 2016 after using the process successfully with clients for a decade.

Yet, while most indictors pointed to me having grown through tragedy and achieved a successful life—including marriage since 1971, a healthy family (including three grandchildren), successful career and comfortable semi-retirement, good overall health, and a general state of happiness—I still had a form of reactive high blood pressure. Engaging in meditation, relaxation, breath work, etc. prior to getting it taken at a medical office did not help. I could not pass my blood pressure test. I was even beginning to believe it because I was becoming "anxious" whenever I thought of going to get it taken. Yet, something significant was changing fairly quickly because I was experiencing a heightened sense of wellbeing when doing other challenging activities.

The data I had gathered so far made me question if there is a difference between an altered trait, whereby some continuous state of improved homeostasis of physiology develops verses an improved voluntary ability to regulate one's reactions when something happens that causes stress and negative emotions. Not being able to pass my blood pressure test in a medical office indicated that I become stressed in nonthreatening situations. Stress responses can "become deregulated and cause pathophysiologic consequences. Another way to think about it is that acute stress is considered to enhance immunity while chronic stress is now considered to suppress immunity" (Clayton, et al., 1212:204). Therefore, I realized my research had not been completed; instead my research may have just begun. I decided to do an Internet search on the vagus nerve and wellbeing. I discovered the *Uplift* article: "12 Ways to Unlock the Powers of the Vagus Nerve" (Ropp, 2017).

I suggest that anyone who wants to explore the wealth of information on the vagus nerve begin with Ropp's article. The content supports that the vagus nerve is highly involved in how we experience regulation. In summary, the nerve fibers of the vagus nerve innervate most of our internal organs. The pathways between the brain, heart, and gut manage and process emotions. Vagus nerve stimulation has been shown to improve such conditions as anxiety disorder, heart disease, migraines, tinnitus, obesity, alcohol addiction, Alzheimer's, leaky gut, bad blood circulation, mood disorder, and cancer. At first, this may be hard to accept. But if stress is an underlying cause of disease, then returning the body to a heightened state of homeostasis could very likely result in health improvements.

The article also states that electrical stimulation of the vagus nerve is being used to treat people with epilepsy and depression. "Researchers studying the effects of vagus stimulation on epilepsy noticed that patients experienced a second benefit unrelated to seizure reduction: their moods also improved." However, it added that there were other ways to stimulate the vagus nerve that did not involve electrical stimulation but involve toning and strengthening it like a muscle.

The exercises that Ropp includes at the end of the article involve more generalized activities such as positive social relations, drinking cold water, gargling, singing and chanting, massage, laughter, yoga and tai chi, breathing deeply and slowly, exercise, and general relaxation. The article mentions a neurostimulation approach called Nervana, which provides electrical stimulation through the left ear to stimulate the vagus nerve. While there was no mention of direct tactile stimulation of the neck or widening the nostrils, the strategies of gargling, singing, chanting, laughter, and breathing are all exercises used in speech-language therapy for improving a variety of communication skills and the swallow.

So far, I had not found anything that conflicted with *my hypothesis that compression on the neck in the area of the jugular vein triggers a physiological reaction that promotes a state of equilibrium without our awareness and that the vagus nerve is involved.* I had also discovered that, due to practice, widening my nostrils was now working almost as well as the collar to create a sense of greater wellbeing. Yet, I could not find anything in the research that specifically mentioned that the vagus nerve could be stimulated directly through touch. The literature did report that certain behaviors triggered the vagus nerve.

After reading that gargling and laughter stimulated the vagus nerve, and suspecting that the yawn, grunt, and sneeze did as well, I began investigating whether specific nonverbal language behaviors triggered similar muscle tension in the neck. I discovered that specific facial expressions, gestures, body postures, and speech sounds did as well. What nonverbal behaviors do you find generate similar tension in the neck? What would you investigate next?

My next step was to investigate the *ways* that the vagus nerve can be triggered rather than what was happening *when* the vagus nerve is stimulated. I began looking for books on the vagus nerve. The first book I acquired (Rosenberg, 2017) reminded me that the vagus nerve (tenth cranial nerve) does not work alone. At the very least, four other cranial nerves are involved. SLPs know that the five cranial nerves are important for two systems of communication: verbal and nonverbal. Both are essential for successful communication. I became excited when I read that Rosenberg identified five cranial nerves to serve the system of "social engagement." Interpersonal communication involves social engagement.

Interpersonal communication includes expressing our "attitudes, intentions, feelings, thoughts, strategies, and expectations" with others (Apple, 1989:330). It involves social behavior—"Conduct which is influenced by the presence of others" (Nicolosi, et al., 1978:28). The SLP's scope of practice also includes the area of socioemotional competence because it is a foundational parameter of interpersonal communication skills. SLPs "have always been in the business of social change and the promotion of human welfare as a consequence of altering communicative behavior" (Prutting, 1982:132). As I mentioned, communication is both verbal and nonverbal. These are "integrative behaviors" that serve to regulate conduct, influence status, and indicate participation (Turkstra, et al., 2003:117). However, it was new to me that the vagus nerve directly impacted social communicative behaviors beyond vocal fold function.

It was time for me to expand my goals beyond reducing "white coat anxiety." I was beginning to get inspired that vagus nerve activation could be applied to additional practices within the field of speech-language pathology than just voice therapy. As you read on about the cranial nerves, what ideas come to you regarding applying these findings to your field?

Six

THE CRANIAL NERVES OF INTERPERSONAL COMMUNICATION

"Posture can be used to take a stance towards or against or away from the world."
Alan Fogel (2013:196)

My interest in the vagus nerve had shifted to how I might integrate this discovery into my own speech-language pathology practices. I began to search for information on behaviors that directly stimulate the vagus nerve with the intention of experiencing a greater sense of ease, increased focus, and improved interpersonal communication skills. The most current and applicable book I found was *Accessing the Healing Power of the Vagus Nerve* by Stanley Rosenberg (2017). Rosenberg is a "world renown" hands-on body therapist. As I mentioned earlier, he stresses that stimulating the vagus nerve triggers social engagement. Socioemotional competence is a foundational requirement for effective interpersonal communication. Rosenberg reminded me that the vagus nerve works in collaboration with four other cranial nerves to accomplish successful interpersonal communication.

According to Rosenberg (2017), five cranial nerves must function together for optimal social engagement: V, VII, IX, X, and XI. "When the ventral branch of the vagus nerve and associated four cranial nerves function properly, human beings and other animals enjoy the desirable state of social engagement" (Rosenberg, 2017:40). This is consistent with the cranial nerves that Darley et al. (1975:110) identified to be critical for motor speech. The difference is that Darley et al. included the hypoglossal nerve (cranial nerve XII) as being important as well. The glossopharyngeal nerve (cranial nerve IX) was not included for motor speech, but Darley et al. identified its importance in elevating the larynx for pitch change. However, Darley et al. called cranial nerve IX the stylopharyngeus nerve. This meant it was time for me to acquire a new book on neuroanatomy for current information on the cranial nerves.

According to Crossman and Neary (2015:108-109), cranial nerve five (CNV) is the trigeminal nerve, which has both sensory and motor components. It is the primary sensory nerve of the head and has three divisions of sensory fibers: mandibular, maxillary, and ophthalmic. The face and scalp, the cornea, and the nasal and oral cavities (including the teeth, gums, and paranasal sinuses) relay sensations of touch, pressure, pain and temperature. Fibers terminate in the thalamus, which sends fibers to the parietal lobe, the pathway of "conscious awareness." Fibers also go to the cerebellum and brainstem to trigger grimacing and eye closure as protective reflexes. Sensory fibers from the nasal mucosa are involved with the sneeze and cough reflex due to indirect connections with diaphragmatic and stomach muscles.

The motor functions of CNV include the lowering and raising of the jaw for chewing. The masseter and temporalis close the jaw and the lateral and medial pterygoids open the jaw. CNV also innervates the tensor tympani in the middle ear, the mylohyoid, and the anterior belly of the digastric muscle (Crossman and Neary, 2015:107-109). According to Kapit and Elson (1993), the temporalis and masseter muscles are often contracted at times of stress, causing the jaw to clench with the individual unaware. These muscles can easily be palpated when contracted. Clench your jaw. What do you feel when you palpate your neck?

The medial and lateral pterygoids move the jaw forward as well as open it. The pterygoids are within the infratemporal fossa and cannot be palpated (Kapit and Elson, 1993:39). The digastric muscle depresses the mandible and elevates the hyoid bone (Palmer, 1972). The mylohyoid elevates the hyoid bone, the larynx, and the tongue. The tensor tympani muscle pulls the malleus medially and tenses the tympanic membrane reflexively to protect the ear from loud noises. Darley et al. (1975:111), state that this nerve "regulates mouth opening by mandibular movement for all sounds." Do you hear anything when you clench the jaw?

Cranial nerve seven (CNVII) is the facial nerve, which tenses and relaxes the face. "It not only communicates different emotions, but also reflects our internal states in terms of health and wellness" (Rosenberg, 2017:14). The facial nerve contains sensory, motor, and parasympathetic components. Ascending fibers go to the thalamus, which sends fibers to the sensory cortex of the parietal lobe. The sensory fibers sense taste from the anterior two thirds of the tongue, sensations from the floor of the mouth and palate, and skin sensations from the external ear. What do you feel in your neck when you cup your hand behind your ears?

"Motor fibres are distributed to muscles of facial expression, platysma, stylohyoid, the posterior belly of the digastric muscle, and the stapedius muscle of the middle ear" (Crossman and Neary, 2015:110). The facial nerve receives sensory fibers from the brainstem and cerebral cortex, which are involved in mediating protective reflex reactions of the eye to sight and touch and the contraction of the stapedius to loud sounds. According to Rosenberg (2017:14), the stapedius also reduces the sound of our own voice as well as frequencies above and below the human voice. CNV and CNVII serve in listening to and understanding speech. By CNVII sensing the movement and position of our own facial expressions, we actually become engaged with the speaker. "This is crucial to facilitating social engagement" (Rosenberg, 2017:15). What do you feel in your neck when you wince?

Corticobulbar fibers from the motor cortex of the parietal lobe innervate the facial muscles. The muscles of the upper face (frontalis, orbicularis oculi, procerus, corrugator supercilii) are innervated by fibers that are distributed bilaterally, while the fibers going to muscles of the lower face are crossed. "Unilateral upper motor neurone lesions therefore, give rise to paralysis of the lower facial muscles" (Crossman and Neary, 2015:110). Facial muscles below the orbicularis oculi include the nasalis, levator labii superioris, levator anguli oris, levator labii superioris, zygomaticus major, zygomaticus minor, orbicularis oris, risorius, depressor labii inferioris, mentalis, and platysma (Kapit and Elson, 1993). Parasympathetic fibers innervate the submandibular and sublingual salivary glands, the lacrimal gland, and the nasal and oral mucous membranes (Crossman and Neary, 2015:111). According to Darley et al. (1975:111) this nerve modifies lip shape for production of labial consonants and vowels. What do you feel when you press your lips together firmly?

The ninth cranial nerve (CNIX) is the glossopharyngeal nerve. It is primarily a sensory nerve, but there are a few motor fibers. It receives sensations from the "pharynx, the posterior portion of the tongue, eustachian tube, middle ear, taste buds for the pharynx and posterior third of the tongue, chemoreceptors in the carotid body and baroreceptors in the carotid sinus" (Crossman and Neary 2015:112). It has an important function in "mediating the swallow and gag reflex through connections with the hypoglossal muscles." According to Rosenberg (2017:15), CNIX receives sensory input from the tonsils, pharynx, the middle ear, and the posterior third of the tongue. It assists in regulating blood pressure by monitoring blood pressure in order to "influence the heart and the tonus muscles in the arteries. This nerve also monitors oxygen and carbon dioxide levels in the blood to adjust breathing." It also stimulates the "parotid gland, the large salivary gland in front of the ear" (Rosenberg, 2017:15).

Motor function innervates the stylopharyngeus for the swallow. According to Palmer (1972:89), the stylopharyngeus functions to elevate the entire pharynx and widen it superiorly in order for the bolus to be received within the pharynx. A dysphagia therapy strategy to promote a swallow is to press gently on each side of the larynx in a similar location as the Neuro Shield. It made sense to me that the same pressure with the fingertips could produce a greater sense of calm and even lower blood pressure when no threat is present.

The vagus nerve, cranial nerve ten (CNX), contains afferent, motor, and parasympathetic fibers. Crossman and Neary (2015:114) wrote very little about the vagus nerve. Sensory fibers receive general sensations from the pharynx, larynx, esophagus, tympanic membrane, external auditory meatus, and part of the concha of the external ear. There are chemoreceptors in the aortic bodies and baroreceptors in the aortic arch. Receptors are widely distributed through the thoracic and abdominal viscera. The motor fibers innervate the muscles of the soft palate, pharynx, larynx, and upper part of the esophagus; these are "crucially important for the control of speech and swallowing." "Motor fibers arise from the nucleus ambiguus of the medulla. Caudal motor fibers (tail portion) of the vagus nerve "transfer to the vagus nerve proper at the level of the jugular foramen. . . . The parasympathetic fibers of the vagus nerve originate in the dorsal motor nucleus of the vagus, which lies in the medulla immediately beneath the floor of the fourth ventricle. They distributed widely throughout the cardiovascular, respiratory, and gastrointestinal system" (Crossman and Neary, 2015:114).

Kapit and Elson (1993:144) organized information about CNX into four areas. There are special visceral afferents (sensory) from taste receptors at the base of the tongue and epiglottis. There are general somatic receptors for the external ear and external auditory canal. There are general visceral afferents from the pharynx, larynx, thoracic, and abdominal viscera. There are general visceral efferents (innervate muscles) from the parasympathetic system to muscles of the thoracic and abdominal viscera.

Rosenberg (2017) identified two branches of CNX: the ventral vagus nerve and the dorsal vagus nerve (originating from the dorsal motor nucleus in the brainstem). He stressed that it is essential to understand the two branches in order to devise treatment options for a wide variety of health issues. More on these two branches, including an introduction of the Polyvagal Theory by psychologist Stephen Porges, Ph.D., is at the end of this chapter and is covered more fully in Chapter Six. Rosenberg explains that the dorsal vagus nerve has motor fibers that innervate the organs below the diaphragm. They run from the stomach to the "ascending and transverse segments of the colon." Some dorsal vagus fibers also affect the heart and lungs. The ventral vagus nerve's motor pathways are primarily above the diaphragm, yet some influence organs below the diaphragm. "All three parts of the autonomic nervous system—the dorsal vagus and ventral branches of the vagus nerve, and the spinal sympathetic chain—affect the vital functions of breathing and blood circulation" (Rosenberg, 2017:19).

Cranial nerve eleven (CNXI) is the accessory nerve, which is "one of the keys to the well-being of the entire musculoskeletal system. Because it innervates the trapezius and sternocleidomastoid muscles, which enable movement of the head and neck, tension in either of these muscles on one side, pulls the shoulder, spine, and the entire system out of alignment" (Rosenberg, 2017:20). According to Crossman and Neary (2015:115), this nerve is only motor. Nerve fibers travel through the jugular foramen and are then "distributed to the muscles of the soft palate, pharynx, and larynx." Once leaving the jugular foramen, the fibers "join the vagus and are distributed with it. . . . Fibers of the spinal root pass to the sternomastoid and trapezius muscles, which serve the head and shoulders." The sternocleidomastoid muscle tilts the head laterally while rotating it and pulling the head downward as well as lifting the chin and rotating the head to the opposite side (Kapit and Elson, 1993).

Cranial nerves IX (glossopharyngeal), X (ventral and dorsal portions of the vagus nerve), and XI (accessory nerve) are closely woven together along with the jugular vein. They all pass through the jugular foramen. This relationship relates to what I originally discovered about the Neuro Shield collar putting pressure on the jugular vein. The pressure creates a higher "fluid" barrier between the skull and brain to prevent slosh. As mentioned, it produces a similar effect as the yawn. Yet those researches said that the function of the yawn is unknown. In the initial video, reporter Danni Washington wore the Neuro Shield while doing a gross motor concentration task. She stated that her performance improved (Washington, n.d.). What is important to note is that while the ventral vagus nerve is highly involved in calming the nervous system and promoting social engagement, the entire system is highly interconnected. I was becoming even more convinced that this system could be activated through specific voluntary movements involving the five cranial nerves.

The head and neck is very important for body postures, which can generate either a positive or negative mood. According to psychologist and University of Utah professor Alan Fogel (2013:195, 196), even in the early 1980's "experimental subjects who were placed in hunched and threatened physical postures reported feeling more depressed. . . . Posture is our way of expressing the basic biobehavioral response modes" of the sympathetic and parasympathetic nervous system. "Posture can be *used* to take a stance towards [engagement] or against [fight mobilization] or away [flight mobilization] from the world."

The important word here is "used," which indicates that posture can actually be utilized as a "tool" to affect how the nervous system reacts to circumstances. Pressing on the sides of the neck may actually be a "tool" that triggers an instinctive movement that aligns the head and neck back into a sociably engaged "stance." I had already observed that certain facial expressions produced similar tension in the neck. I learned that these behaviors serve as a form of "vagal breaking."

Rosenberg's explanation of the tenth cranial nerve (CNX) included a theory on the role of the vagus nerve in the autonomic nervous system. It is called the Polyvagal Theory, which was introduced by Stephen Porges, Ph.D. in the 1900's. Porges's theory identifies the importance of these cranial nerves' interactions with the vagus nerve (CNX). One aspect of the Polyvagal Theory made great sense to me in regard to certain behaviors being used as "tools" for inhibiting stress responses. The ventral vagus nerve serves as the "vagal brake." This is consistent with what Chowdhary and Townsend (2001:219) wrote about as the "indirect vagal effect."

It is Stephen Porges who first identified the vagus nerve to be the nerve of social engagement (Rosenberg, 2017). What I was reminded of from reviewing these five cranial nerves is that the nerves for speaking, which involve articulation, voice, and fluency, are essential for interpersonal communication among individuals with functional hearing. Facial expressions and postures are even more important for all interpersonal communication. This is covered in Chapter Twelve, "The Theory of Nonverbal Language Integration."

According to the Polyvagal Theory, the entire vagus nerve must be activated for social engagement (thus interpersonal communication) to be successful. Recall that over eighty percent of the fibers of the vagus nerve are afferent viscerosensory fibers (Gudmundsson, 2014:165). The other twenty percent are the motor fibers of the vagus nerve, which innervate the muscles of the larynx, pharynx, soft palate, upper esophagus, heart, lungs, abdominal viscera, and stomach (Greenstein and Greenstein, 2000; Nicolosi et al., 1978, Wilson-Pauwels, et. al. 1988).

Wilson-Pauwels, et al. (1988:128-130) identify three principal motor branches of the vagus nerve. The pharyngeal branch supplies the pharynx and soft palate. The superior laryngeal nerve divides into the internal and external laryngeal nerves. The external laryngeal nerve supplies the cricothyroid muscle to help tense the vocal folds. The third branch is the recurrent laryngeal nerve, which supplies the intrinsic muscles of the larynx. These muscles control the shape of the opening between the vocal folds (glottis), and the length and tension of the vocal folds. The speech-language pathologist's primary concern regarding the vagus nerve has been with these three branches because damage causes voice and swallowing deficits.

Now, I discovered that the entire vagus nerve is important for interpersonal communication because it has a role in inhibiting the sympathetic nervous system. It has an important interrelationship with at least four other cranial nerves that affect facial expression and head and neck posture. Suddenly, the concept of *rapport* came to me. Successful interpersonal communication begins with establishing an accepting, empathetic, and trusting environment. My next step was to acquire a book by Porges on the Polyvagal Theory. The Polyvagal Theory expanded my understanding regarding the relationship between the ventral vagus nerve and rapport.

Seven

THE VENTRAL VAGUS NERVE AND RAPPORT

*"Communication is facilitated when there is capacity to create
a non-evaluative atmosphere."* Dean Barnlund (1973:24)

According to Stephen Porges (2017), the Polyvagal Theory is concerned with the adaptive function of spontaneous behaviors and how these behaviors are involved in regulating our physiological states. Adaptive functions evolve to promote survival, minimize distress, and generate physiological states that help to "optimize health, growth, and restoration" (Porges, 2017:224). Yet, it is what Porges wrote about *maladaptive* behaviors that I could relate to my blood pressure. A maladaptive behavior arises when a behavior that initially enabled a person to overcome acute challenges then becomes activated habitually even when there is no threat. "Such a behavior would be maladaptive, since it would not optimize survival and may compromise physiological function and amplify distress." (Porges, 2017:1).

This gave me a new idea about what was happening with my "white coat anxiety," which caused me to fail my blood pressure tests in medical offices. It may not necessarily be negative subconscious memories that are increasing my stress level. It is possible that it evolved from a reactive behavior that enables me to address acute critical conditions that arise in healthcare. I may not know how to "behave" when I am the patient and, therefore, I become acutely uncomfortable. It may be as simple as not knowing how to be socially engaged with the professional taking my blood pressure. Or it may be the negative connotations or heightened sensitivity to the disciplinary action of an upper arm being gripped. It could also be "all the above."

Porges's description of the social engagement system includes safety-based explanations of the autonomic nervous system. There are somatomotor pathways and visceral efferent pathways. Somatomotor pathways regulate striated muscles [long thin muscles of the skeletal system used for movement]. As I mentioned, SLPs are well aware that nerve pathways for the muscles of the face, head, and neck involve the cranial nerves. The nerves that regulate muscles of the limbs and trunk travel through the spinal column. There are visceral motor nerves within the autonomic nervous system [which will be discussed as per the Polyvagal Theory], "that regulate smooth muscle and cardiac muscles and glands" (Porges, 2017:31).

According to Porges, the social engagement system involves the somatomotor components that regulate the face and head. The visceromotor component regulates the heart and bronchi. "Functionally, the social engagement system emerges from a heart-face connection that coordinates the heart with the muscles of the face and head. The initial function of the system is to coordinate sucking-swallowing-breathing-vocalizing. Atypical coordination of this system early in life is an indicator of subsequent difficulties in social behavior and emotional regulation" (Porges, 2017:27). I would, therefore, add that there is involvement of the neck as well.

I began to wonder how far back my reactive blood pressure might go. While I prefer not to attribute current physiological and emotional challenges to my childhood, I suddenly accepted an influence I had not considered. Growing up as the second-to-the youngest of five siblings in a household whose father was a high school teacher who had stuttered badly as a child (yet spoke fluently), had a Purple Heart due to both upper legs being run over by a tank in World War II (yet walked eighteen-hole golf courses), and who demonstrated anger symptoms (now recognized as post traumatic syndrome) may have caused me to feel uncomfortable with certain people in certain situations. And considering that I recall blushing when I "spoke up" in college classes, I suspect that my discomfort may be with authority figures. Technicians taking my blood pressure are in charge.

Interestingly, Porges shared that his "scientific journey has been a personal quest for an intervening variable that would contribute to our understanding of individual differences in behavior" (Porges, 2017:41). I realized that I was on a scientific journey to understand some universal principal of behavior. It had become a personal quest to understand how neck compression contributes to reducing stress, improving focus, and enhancing a greater sense of ease (poise) while working alone or communicating with others. This means neck compression and certain behaviors are interconnected with interpersonal communication and adjust physiological responses.

The Polyvagal Theory provides a way to explain how physiological states are significant factors that influence our behavior, including how we interact with others. Porges states that threatening and/or risky situations produce defensive physiological states. In order for positive social engagement to occur, there must be a feeling of safety. "The theory explains how safety is not the removal of threat and that feeling safe is dependent on unique cues in the environment and in our relationships that have an active inhibition on defense circuits and promote health and feelings of love and trust" (Porges, 2017:43).

This is what SLPs refer to as rapport. We cannot remove the cause of the problem, but we can help our clients and their families feel safe in the clinical setting. It is important that defense circuits are inhibited. This helps our clients engage in and work on behaviors through facial, oral, pharyngeal, laryngeal, and postural exercises as well as communication and/or swallow strategies that might, otherwise, be socially uncomfortable. More on rapport follows at the end of this chapter.

The Polyvagal Theory offers a different way to view the autonomic nervous system. It focuses on the vagus nerve (CNX), which means "wandering" in Latin. It connects brainstem areas to important internal organs. The autonomic nervous system regulates the internal organs without conscious awareness. Traditionally, this system was divided into two opposite divisions: the sympathetic (fight and flight) and parasympathetic (homeostasis). An antagonist regulation of motor pathways traveling to specific organs was emphasized. The sensory pathways "traveling from the organs to the brain or brainstem areas regulating both sensory and motor pathways that provided the bidirectional communication between internal organs and the brain" were not emphasized (Porges, 2017:5).

The Polyvagal Theory redefines the autonomic system by including sensory pathways and emphasizing the brainstem areas regulating autonomic function. There are three rather than two divisions: the sympathetic nervous system and two pathways that travel through the vagus nerve: ventral vagus and dorsal vagus. I am repeating this to reiterate the differences. According to Porges, the dorsal vagus originates in the dorsal nucleus of the vagus, terminates in the visceral organs below the diaphragm, and is unmyelinated. The ventral vagus originates from the nucleus ambiguous, terminates in the visceral organs above the diaphragm, and is myelinated.

It is the ventral vagus nerve that has the three laryngeal nerve branches within the neck. The ventral vagus nerve has a strong interconnection with the four cranial nerves of the face and head (V, VII, IX, and XI). When these cranial nerves function in a balanced manner, there is "optimal autonomic balance between the sympathetic nervous system and the dorsal vagal pathways to subdiaphragmatic organs" (Porges, 2017:6). When the ventral vagus nerve is dampened, the autonomic nervous system moves to fight or flight through increased sympathetic activity. This activity inhibits the dorsal vagus, which would otherwise result in a "biobehavioral shutdown manifested as depressed sympathetic activation and a surge in the dorsal vagus influences that would result in fainting, defecation, and an inhibition of motor behavior often seen in mammals feigning death."

The ventral vagus nerve is linked to emotional expression through vocalizations, the muscle tone of the upper face and head, and the control of the heart. Porges stresses that states of emotion are revealed in the upper face, the eyes, eyebrows, and forehead. "We look to the upper part of the face for cues of affect. If we block that, then we may misinterpret their emotional response. If we block their vagal control of the heart, since the area of the brainstem regulating the vagus is also regulating the face, then they're going to have problems in social interaction" (Porges, 2017:144). But there is something additional on that page, and I became excited. The "lower part of the face is involved in biting, and part of the defense system associated with fight/flight behaviors." I recalled reading that oculomotor nerve (CNIII), carries automatic parasympathetic efferent fibers (Greenstein and Greenstein, 2000:234). This suggests that eyes are for social engagement while biting is an aggressive act.

I put my hand to my mouth and pretended to bite it. The movements were accomplished with ease. Then, I put light pressure on my neck with my fingertips. It was more difficult to open my jaw to bite. I widened my nares, and again, it required more effort to open my jaw to bite. Then I palpated my neck while widening my nares and felt that familiar bulging of muscles on the sides of my neck. I imagined the expression of happiness in my eyes. It was difficult to bite, and I could feel the familiar muscle tension on the sides of my neck. I palpated my neck as I opened my jaw to bite; there was no slight bulge. I found my husband, Chuck, watching financial programs, interrupted him, and asked him to pretend to bite his arm. Then I put light pressure on his neck and asked him to do it again. He said it was difficult and then laughed. While not sophisticatedly scientific, this data suggested to me that touching the neck and other voluntary actions, such as widening the nostrils, might be triggering the ventral vagus nerve to put a brake on aggression and promote the state of rapport.

Porges identifies two important points underlying the Polyvagal Theory. First, the autonomic nervous system is sending data about the body to the brain. The vagus nerve is the largest nerve in the autonomic nervous system. Recall that eighty percent of its fibers are afferent (sensory). It is the major nerve of the parasympathetic nervous system. A significant amount of the sensory information it collects is from the viscera of the body's organs, which is sent to the brain stem. This is different from data that is sent via the spinal column, which is more specific compared to the diffuseness of the sensations from the viscera, "and the diffuse feelings often 'color' our perceptions and reactions to social interactions" (Porges, 2017:223).

This explanation fits with the "diffuse" feeling of heightened positive mood that I experienced when I touched my neck or widened my nostrils. It also supports what I theorized in my dissertation, which I completed in 2006. "Every event triggers physiological sensations and emotion, be it joy or fear." The facts of an event include "the physiological sensations that resulted at the time of the incident." The impressions from these sensations are "the perceptions of the emotions that occurred at the time" (Bohntinsky, 2016:107, 110).

My dissertation includes a process for transforming loss into opportunities for returning to positive states of mind by labeling experiences through physiological sensations rather than emotions. It shows that there are a limited number of adjectives that describe actual physiological sensations, or feelings. Emotions, on the other hand, could be thought of as impressions of these sensations. They are described by a multitude of positive or negative adjectives depending upon the interpretation of the situation. Physiological feelings can be described with such words as airy, light, charged, heavy, or constricting. Emotions have descriptive adjectives from A to Z, angry or affable to zealous.

Acknowledging physiological sensations as "facts" helps to circumvent judgment when blaming one's self or others is not fully warranted. A more positive state of mind returns. This state enhances the ability to determine a better course of action if a similar situation were to arise again. The Polyvagal Theory helped me realize that this process was activating the ventral vagus nerve. Yet, activation was indirect through a critical thinking process that integrated awareness of sensations, intrapersonal communication (inner speech), and metacognition (awareness of cognitive states).

Porges's second point is that past research primarily focused on ventral vagus nerve functions in relationship to motor control of the autonomic nervous system. This is the motor control of the organs depending on information from neural pathways in the periphery (the senses) in order to resume homeostasis. However, the dorsal vagus nerve is involved with the autonomic nervous system's defense system from a very early phylogenic perspective of immobilization, which is seen in reptiles. The sympathetic nervous system of fight/fight and the parasympathetic nervous systems of homeostasis have long been considered to be antagonistic and the only options of the autonomic nervous system.

The Polyvagal Theory sees all three to be interacting in a hierarchical manner. "This functional hierarchy mirrors the phylogeny of the autonomic components of vertebrates" (Porges, 2017:226). The ventral vagus nerve function was the last to evolve. I realized that there are many situations where we go from being immobilized by an event and then may move into a fight or flight stance before returning to a state of homeostasis. Porges theorizes that this activation happens below our level of perception and calls the process "neuroception." "Neuroception is the nervous system's evaluation of risk in the environment without conscious awareness" (Porges, 2017: 143). That means it occurs without any metacognition or self talk.

Neuorception actually offered a term regarding what could be happening from the compression collar, touching the sides of the neck, and the yawn. Something is happening below the level of conscious awareness in order for these "tools" to inhibit the autonomic nervous system from becoming immobilized or moving into fight or flight. Through neuroception, certain behaviors may automatically prepare the mind and body to focus, attend, and perform. This suggests that certain behaviors are *tools* that can help establish rapport prior to evidence-based therapeutic interventions.

According to Geller and Foley (2009:7) rapport in speech-language pathology relates to relationship-based interventions and is about being "warm, engaging, and friendly." They define rapport as an "emotional bond or friendly relationship between individuals based on mutual liking, trust, and a sense that they are understood and share each other's concerns" (Geller and Foley, 2009:15). Relationship-based interventions see the caregivers as the "agents of change" and the "strengths and capacities" of the caregivers and the client are "key elements for change and growth." In relationship-based interventions, the SLP has a responsibility to "empower" clients and caregivers to recognize their own capacities in ways that improve self-confidence (Geller and Foley, 2009:7).

So much was beginning to make sense to me in regard to the interconnections between the vagus nerve, homeostasis, rapport, and direct activation. I searched for the word "rapport" in the multitude of clinical books I had acquired since 1974. Rapport was only in the index of two. Another text did not list rapport, but states that "communication is facilitated when there is capacity to create a non-evaluative atmosphere" (Barnlund, 1971:24). Barnlund quoted Carl Roger's suggestion that the "major barrier to interpersonal communication is our very natural tendency to judge, to evaluate, to approve, or disprove the statement of another or group."

Vinson (1999:100) defined rapport to be a "harmonious connection between two individuals based on mutual respect and a level of trust." Clients need to know that they are being understood as a person not just a clinical case. Vinson also identified enthusiasm to be a critical element. Perkins (1971:375) stressed the importance of establishing rapport before engaging in therapy techniques. Through "acceptance and goodwill" resistance to a diagnosis and remediation strategies is reduced and cooperation is enlisted.

Rapport, however, is not just about harmony being achieved with others through friendliness, acceptance, supportiveness, and competency. I now understood that it is about helping clients and caregivers achieve optimal interpersonal communication during every session. Rapport helps them experience their strengths and capacities for being their own agents of change for growth. I now realized what innervating the ventral vagus nerve was improving my grandchildren's and my ability to establish rapport. We are consciously and voluntarily becoming our own agents of change. This fit well with what Geller and Foley called "working from the inside out." Vagus nerve activation could actually generate authentic levels of rapport in ways that optimize learning and enhance outcomes from evidence-based interventions in clinical situations.

From this perspective, rapport could be expanded beyond interpersonal communication between individuals because it would involve facilitating a non-evaluative atmosphere within one's self. I was now convinced that the ventral vagus nerve for homeostasis and social engagement could be activated, exercised, and toned directly through certain behaviors. There was so much more that I wanted to explore, but it was time to change my focus away from the research literature. Now, I wanted to know what other natural behaviors activated the ventral vagus nerve. I turned back to the work of Rosenberg (2017), which provided some simple exercises for innervating the ventral vagus nerve. Doing the exercises brought my thinking full circle and back to the yawn.

Eight

THE COMPLEXITY OF THE YAWN

"These neurotransmitters regulate pleasure, sensuality, and relationship bonding between individuals, so if you want to enhance your intimacy and stay together, then yawn together."   Andrew Newberg and Mark Robert Walden (2010:158)

Body worker Stanley Rosenberg (2017) provided simple exercises for innervating the ventral vagus nerve. The instructions for one exercise are to lie on the floor and hold a lateral eye position to the right until there is a yawn or sigh. Repeat by holding the lateral eye position in the left until a sigh or yawn. When I did the exercise, I noticed there was similar tension in my neck muscles although lighter than the tension produced by the yawn and the sigh. I decided to turn my investigation back to the yawn because it was mentioned in the article about the Q Collar. The compression collar stimulates the omohyoid muscle and produces a similar response as the yawn. These interconnections began this entire investigation in July 2018.

Coherent scientific information on yawning in regards to physiology, functions, and applications comes from the work of Newberg and Waldman (2010). Andrew Newberg, M.D. works at Myrna Brind Center of Integrative Medicine and Thomas Jefferson University Hospital and Sidney Kimmel Medical College. Mark Robert Waldman teaches "Neuroleadership" at Loyola Marymount University. Together, they write on the interface between spirituality and neuroscience. The authors stressed the importance of including the yawn in "preparatory" warm-up activities, and their most general conclusion about the yawn is that it "relaxes the mind" (Newberg and Waldman, 2017:195).

Newberg and Waldman's basic observation is that the yawn is a "powerful neural-enhancing tool." The yawn stimulates the precuneus, which is a small structure within the parietal lobe. It has a central role in consciousness, self-reflection, and memory retrieval. Conscious deep breathing also stimulates the precuneus (Newberg and Waldman, 2010, 155-156). [More on the precuneus follows in this chapter.] They stressed that the yawn is so effective and important to the functioning of the brain that they asked the reader to review the thirty-four yawn-related studies cited in the endnotes. I did review many of those studies, and I found additional ones as well.

One related finding is in the abstract of a 2015 study in "Dysphagia." Kimiko, et al. (2015) found that the yawn played a role in eliciting the rest swallow—or swallow of saliva. According to the abstract, the yawn involves deep inhalation, dilation of the respiratory track, wide jaw opening, and a facial grimace. The yawn can be elicited by seeing or hearing another yawn or by thinking about the yawn, a phenomenon known as "contagious yawning." "The yawn is mediated by a distributed network of brainstem and 'supratentorial' brain regions, the components which are shared with other airway behaviors including respiration, swallowing, and mastication." The subtentorial brain includes the cerebrum (frontal, parietal, temporal and occipital lobes) and the diencephalon (the area of the thalamus, hypothalamus, and pituitary gland), which is involved in the control of hormones. By palpating my neck, I observed that the yawn produced the greatest amount of tension in the same location as swallowing, mastication, exaggerated voluntary quick inhalation, and blowing.

These researchers found that swallows automatically followed elicited yawns and that sixty-five percent of the rest swallows (saliva) occurred within ten seconds after a yawn. This "temporal coupling" between the yawn and swallow indicates that they are interrelated physiologically and neurologically. These "novel" findings now extend the "current model" of the neurophysiology of the "upper airway." Moreover, the researchers pointed out that this data shows the possibility that the yawn "plays a role in eliciting the rest swallow." This made great sense to me because tactile stimulation on the sides of the larynx is a facilitation technique in swallowing therapy. Earlier I had observed that I produced more "rest swallows" in one minute when I touched the sides of my larynx. I decided that these findings offered a good rationale for including the elicitation of the yawn in swallowing therapy exercises, especially when focusing on the "dry" swallow (saliva). I wanted to research what more had been discovered about the relationships between the yawn and swallow.

Ertekin, et al. (2015: 2073-80) investigated the "electrophysiological" association between the spontaneous yawn and swallow. Three phases of the yawn were identified. The first involves "opening the mouth, dilation of the pharynx, larynx and thorax and lowering of the diaphragm muscle." The second phase involves the modifications of facial expression, which includes exaggerated mouth opening and closing of the eyes. Neck stretching occurs along with "trunk extension including hyperextension of limb muscles." In the third phase, inspiration stops, a slow expiration follows, and all structures resume their "usual aspects." The duration of the yawn has been timed by researchers to be between four and ten seconds.

Their study investigated the yawns of fifteen healthy subjects, ten individuals with Parkinson's disease, and ten individuals with brainstem stroke. Yawns and swallows were identified using "l-h polygraphic recording." Of the 132 yawns recorded, 113 yawns (86.6%) were associated with spontaneous swallows either "during the yawn period and swallows just after or within 2 s [two seconds] following the yawn." This was the most frequent. Ertekin et al. acknowledged that there was no clear evidence regarding why the yawn and spontaneous swallow of saliva are associated but added that increased saliva production in association with yawning has been reported.

Ertekin et al. (2015) identified two types of yawning: spontaneous and contagious. Both types are similar in terms of motor behavior and the triggering mechanisms. For both, a coordinated effort is coming from the cranial nerves (CNV, CNVII, IX, X, XI, and XII), intercostal nerves, and pathways linked to respiratory rhythm. What was becoming very evident to me is interrelationship. The six cranial nerves identified in Chapter Four to be important for interpersonal communication are also involved in the yawn, which then triggers the swallow with high consistency.

Besides the lower motor neuron involvement (cranial nerves), the yawn also innervates the cerebral cortex, especially the precuneus. Platek et al. (2005) discovered from fMRIs (functional magnetic resonance imaging) that viewing someone yawn evokes neural activity in the posterior cingulate and precuneus. The researchers concluded that the yawn is involved with empathy, but cautioned that this theory receives conflicting results in the literature.

Newberg and Waldman (2010) had concluded that the yawn did much more and briefly mentioned the precuneus. Cavanna and Trimble (2006) provided a very rich review of the anatomy and function of the precuneus based on peer-reviewed neuroimaging studies in the literature. Prior to the availability of neuroimaging, the precuneus (or the mesial extent of Brodmann's area 7), had been a difficult area to study. It is buried in the interhemispheric fissure as well as encased by veins. This review article offers exciting support for the yawn being a neural enhancing tool because it activates the precuneus.

The precuneus is the medial portion of the posterior parietal lobe. It belongs to the "associative cortices" and assists the brain in "integrating both external and self-generated information to produce much of the mental activity that characterizes Homo sapiens" (Cavanna and Trimble, 2006:568). The precuneus has a role in motor imagery (imagined movement) and the spatial attention required for whole body movements. It is also involved in the cognitive tasks of "visual rotation, deductive reasoning, music processing, and mental navigation." Functional imaging studies have shown music processing and visual imagery to be closely interconnected. It also has a role in attentional shifts between object features whether requiring actual vision or imagery. Neuroimaging has also shown that "it is likely that different aspects of episodic memory retrieval are represented in distinct regions of the precuneus" (Cavanna and Trimble, 2006: 575). Episodic memory involves recalling those events (interactions with people, places, and things) that have affected us personally.

I became even more excited about the potentiality of the yawn, as well as other behaviors that may actually activate the system that triggers the precuneus. Wallace (2007) discusses where the psychological practices of Buddhism interface with the neurophysiology of Western medicine. Suddenly, I saw an interconnection between the central aims of mindfulness in regard to the precuneus, compassion, and rapport. "Compassion is based on empathy, but in a very deep sense, insight into the nature of oneself, others, and the relation between oneself and the rest of the world is also synergistically related to empathy" (Wallace, 2007:114). While this is not the place to address the rich complexity of the precuneus and its relationship to the attributes of compassion and rapport such as attention, imagery, reasoning, and memory, I did wonder what might happen if clinicians began each treatment session with the yawn.

I searched ASHA's publications regarding what had been discovered about the precuneus. That led me to the article: "The Cortical Mechanisms of Speech Perception in Noise" (Wong, et al., 2008:1026). Although nothing significant was mentioned about the precuneus, I could entertain an additional possibility of what might be happening in relationship to the yawn. "Verbal communication in the modern world often occurs in the presence of interfering background noise. As such, listeners must develop sensory, cognitive, and neural resources for handling noise to achieve successful speech processing and communication. . . . Reduced ability for understanding speech in a noise is a primary symptom of (central) auditory processing disorder." I yawned and heard soft popping and rumbling sounds.

I recalled that cranial nerves V, VII, XI and X were involved in protecting the ears from loud noises. Cranial nerve XI innervates the neck muscles involved in ducking the head away from loud noises. What I found of particular importance is that neural resources can be developed to filter out distractions in order to improve the ability to process what is important. This concept fits with what I had been observing about myself since I began "exercising" the vagus nerve with a collar, by using my fingertips to create light tactile pressure on the sides of my neck, by widening my nostrils, and with lateral eye movements. I may have an improved ability to process what is important because noises are being filtered out. One very notable change is that distracting noises were no longer bothering me as much.

Wong et al. (2008) investigated the "neural/cortical" areas associated with listening to speech in noise in younger adults with normal auditory functions. The results showed that listening to speech in a moderately noisy condition activates a more extensive brain network than in quiet. This network includes Wernicke's area. It is the major area involved in the comprehension of language as well as a critical structure in social cognition, which is on the left side of the brain in most people. "Activation was also found in the inferior parietal region and middle frontal gyrus. In addition, attentional areas (e.g. cingulate gyrus, medial frontal gyrus) as well as subcortical structures (basal ganglia and thalamus) were activated . . . as well as an extensive auditory-attentional network" (Wong et al., 2008:1033).

These researchers included the left superior temporal gyrus, additional parietal and frontal cerebral cortex regions (including the inferior parietal lobule), lateral prefrontal cortex, and left anterior insular cortex. Wong et al. (2008: 1035, 1037) concluded that "relative to listening to speech in quiet, listening to speech in noise resulted in increased brain activation in a network of brain areas, including the auditory cortex. . . . Activation in these brain regions, including the bilateral auditory cortex, the thalamus, the cingulate gyrus, and various frontal areas, suggest the recruitment of additional neural resources for extracting the speech signal in the presence of noise." Cranial nerves V, VII, IX, and X are participants in this process. It has also been established that the yawn requires the activation of these cranial nerves and the yawn activates the limbic system.

While it was neuoranatomist Pierre Paul Broca who first described a border (limbus) as "the ring of gyri that surround the brainstem," it was neuroscientist James Papez who introduced the limbic system in 1937. Papez described a circuit of emotion, called the Circuit of Papez (Greenstein and Greenstein, 2000:316). At that time, the Circuit of Papez initially included the "hypothalamus, mammillary bodies, anterior thalamic nuclei, cingulate gyrus, and hippocampal formation." Later, neuroscience expanded this circuitry to include the "septal area, the nucleus accumbens, and neocortical areas including the amygdala and orbitofrontal cortex."

"The limbic structures are phylogenetically very ancient, and the hippocampal formation includes a primitive form of cortex underlying the evolutionary newer neocortex" (Greenstein and Greenstein, 2000:316). The limbic system's gray matter (contains cell nuclei and interneurons) includes the "limbic lobe, the hippocampal formation, the amygdaloidal nucleus, and the anterior nucleus of the thalamus. The connecting pathways of the system are the alveus, fimbria, fornix, mamillothalamic tract and the stria terminalis." According to Papez's hypothesis, there is reciprocal communication between higher cognitive centers of the brain and the hypothalamus, "an area that generates such emotions as rage." From the Polyvagal Theory perspective, the hypothalamus's heightened output would not be the emotion of rage, but the sympathetic nervous systems heightened state of fight or flight. The other response is immobilization, which may be more passive aggressive.

While the limbic system is an expansive field of study beyond the intention of this guidebook, I reviewed another area that the yawn stimulates: the cingulate gyrus. The cingulate gyrus is "intimately involved" in the functions of the limbic system. It is considered to be a "form of primitive cortex" with three layers (Greenstein and Greenstein, 2000:326). The cingulate gyrus is in "continuity" with the parahippocampal gyrus. The "hippocampal formation" is severely atrophied in Alzheimer's disease, "leading to amnesia for relatively recent events and the inability to learn new information of an autobiographical kind, i.e. loss of episodic memory" (Crossman and Neary, 2015:167). The main efferent output is from the anterior thalamic nuclei to the cingulate gyrus, and responses generated by the cingulate gyrus are "automatic, somatic, or behavioral depending on the site of stimulation."

According to Greenstein and Greenstein (2000:326), innervation of the cingulate gyrus stimulates respiration, salivation, pupillary dilatation, bladder contraction, the inhibition of peristalsis, and elevates or depresses blood pressure (which is regulated by the ventral vagus nerve). This offers an explanation regarding the close association between the yawn and the spontaneous swallow of saliva. Yet, the cingulate gyrus is involved with emotions as well. Behavioral reactions from research on animals have shown that stimulation of the cingulate gyrus ceases activity and causes "seeming" surprise.

"Stimulation of the posterior cingulate gyrus appears to produce pleasurable emotions in contrast to aversive behaviors observed after stimulation of the amygdala. Somatic effects in humans include the inhibition of spontaneous activity in order to inhibit or facilitate reflexive responses (Greenstein and Greenstein, 2000:326). The yawn stimulates the posterior cingulate gyrus, which has been shown to be involved in generating pleasurable sensations and inhibiting distracting behaviors (Newberg and Waldman, 2010:155-159). Thus, the yawn, and other related behaviors, may reset the autonomic nervous system through the Circuit of Papez to optimize automatic, somatic, and behavioral states that promote episodic memory, which is important for learning. It appears that, in the very least, these behaviors would enhance rapport.

Wong et al. (2008) found that listening to speech in a highly noisy condition activated these regions within the limbic system but with greater intensity than less noise. Also, additional parietal and frontal regions showed greater activation, including the inferior parietal lobule, the lateral prefrontal cortex, and the left anterior insular cortex. According to Porges, another contributor to innervating the ventral vagus nerve is listening (2017:76-78). Low frequencies can activate the sympathetic nervous system needed for survival. Low frequency sounds are equated to hearing a large predator. Porges gives the example of hearing footsteps behind us. The attention focused on threatening low frequencies interferes with the ability to hear the high frequency sounds required for understanding speech and intonation patterns. Porges explains that when the focus is on the low frequencies due to being in threatening environments, attention to high frequencies for speech is depressed. On the other hand, positive facial expression combined with an engaging voice contracts the muscles of the middle ear to augment hearing of speech in noisy environments. This information also fits with the possibility that exercising the vagus nerve directly through certain behaviors improves the ability to process what is important because distractions have been filtered out.

As with any research, past studies are addressed, additional resources are suggested, and areas for additional research are recommended. I realized that my investigation of the literature regarding the limbic system and vagus nerve could be an endless process. So far, I had not found any research that disproved my *evolving hypothesis that the ventral vagus nerve could be directly stimulated by touch and specific voluntary behaviors in ways that resulted in enhanced rapport.* Decreased stress results in increased focus, improved interpersonal communication skills, and enhanced learning. I had no idea at the time that I would change this hypothesis into a theory called Nonverbal Language Integration.

I decided it was time to stop researching the literature in regard to the functions of the yawn and turn to exploring other ways to activate the ventral vagus nerve directly. Two research articles regarding two strategies in therapy programs for adults with aphasia confirmed that this was an important direction for my focus. However, it was not the findings about the strategies that inspired me to continue. It was Kurkland et al.'s (2012:S66) astute description of the complexity of human behaviors and language. Their description made me realize that research regarding the correlations between activating the ventral vagus nerve, rapport, and learning could be never ending. Findings will continue to provoke new questions that inspire exploration, research, and discovery within a variety of fields and professions. Kurkland et al.'s paragraph is what inspired me to create this guidebook for clinicians. I would not know how to capture so much so succinctly.

It has become clear that as with all human behaviors, language functions are complex, with normal variability across individuals and across the life span and exceptionally variable responses to brain damage. Indeed, even a "simple" linguistic task such as picture naming, as it is administered in typical aphasia tests, requires the integration of perceptual, semantic, phonological, and articulatory processes that involve multiple feedforward and feedback intra- and interhemispheric circuits to seamlessly coordinate conceptual processing; lexical retrieval; and articulatory planning, initiation, execution, and monitoring. Moreover, if the names or descriptions of objects are used in natural conversation, as is typically done in the context of informing others, requesting an object, or asking a question, a multitude of additional factors relating to the common knowledge of interacting individuals; their intentions, affective–emotional states, and beliefs; and the interaction context play an important role. At the level of brain function, this implies a well-tuned interaction between linguistic neural systems with motor and sensory circuits, as well as systems for memory, planning, and emotion. Therefore, the wider cognitive brain systems can, in theory, hinder or facilitate the linguistic machinery.

I had been doing the lateral eye exercise, voluntary yawning, and widening my nostrils regularly. My observations continued to support that these behaviors were activating "brain systems" that facilitated attention and enhanced outcomes. My husband, Chuck, is highly resistant to any of my "helpful" suggestions for self-improvement and generally refuses to participate in any of my "experiments." However, he had noticed the positive changes in me since wearing my compression collar and stimulating my vagus nerve through specific behaviors. He agreed to practice yawning after reading the pages about the purpose of the yawn by Newberg and Walden (2010).

The authors identified the neurochemicals that are involved in the yawning process. These include "dopamine, which activates production in your hypothalamus and hippocampus, areas essential for memory recall, voluntary control, and temperature regulation. These neurotransmitters regulate pleasure, sensuality, and relationship bonding between individuals, so if you want to enhance your intimacy and stay together, then yawn together" (Newberg and Walden, 2010: 158). They identify twelve essential reasons to yawn.

> *Stimulates alertness and concentration.*
> *Optimizes brain activity and metabolism.*
> *Improves cognitive function.*
> *Increases memory recall.*
> *Enhances consciousness and introspection.*
> *Lowers stress.*
> *Relaxes every part of your body.*
> *Improves voluntary muscle control.*
> *Enhances athletic skills.*
> *Fine tunes your sense of time.*
> *Increases empathy and social awareness.*
> *Enhances pleasure and sensuality.*

At first, Chuck could not yawn voluntarily or contagiously to my yawn. I realized that I did not recall ever seeing him yawn, but he often commented on mine. I encouraged him to keep practicing. A day later, I heard him announce, "I yawned." We began to play-act yawning into each other's faces. The next day, I went for a long walk and he went to the gym; neither of us are enthusiastic exercisers. When he came back from the gym he announced, "I do not know why but for some reason I was really motivated today." He talked about using the exercise machines with greater ease and even working out on more machines than usual. Now, if I could only use one behavior to establish rapport before a treatment session, it would be the yawn.

Nine

INTUITION

And this internal voice, which is committed to helping us survive and prosper, is heard and obeyed often on a subconscious level even when survival is not immediately threatened.

An idea began to emerge from the combination of objective research of the literature and my observations from ethological explorations. I still wondered how it was that the yawn, and other behaviors that very likely, stimulate the ventral vagus nerve in the same way, accomplish the twelve positive outcomes identified by Newberg and Waldman (2010:158). Thinking about Kurkland et al.'s (2012: S66) "linguistic machinery," I realized that a powerful behavior that can sabotage all twelve outcomes is negative language whether verbal or nonverbal. A powerful behavior that can enhance all twelve is positive language. One of the most important behaviors that can be either inspirational or detrimental in accomplishing goals is how we talk to ourselves – the "linguistic machinery" of internal or intrapersonal communication.

Intrapersonal communication involves semantics (the actual words we say) and a sense of the intonation of the "inner voice's" expression. It can trigger facial expression, gestures, and postures. Sometimes thoughts can be so detrimental as to create permanent frown lines on the face and change posture. Dwelling on fearful thoughts can build resistance to trying anything new. There are many books written on ways to promote positive thinking (or positive self talk). Some involve mindfulness activities such as meditation, neurolinguistic programing, and/or voluntary body posturing. I had been trained in many while getting my D.Min. at Wisdom University in San Francisco and attending the Chaplaincy Institute for Interfaith Ministries in Berkeley. My doctoral dissertation is about identifying sensations differently and reframing negative internal communication when loss happens. I taught many of the strategies to my clients and their caregivers as part of speech-language therapy.

Yet, even though I have learned a variety of mindfulness techniques, there are still occasions when my thoughts can cause some form of over reactiveness. In particular, just thinking the words "blood pressure test" seemed to trigger tension and could even make me shudder. Other words on different topics could provoke me as well. Yet, I realized certain kinds of unnecessary "warning" thoughts had significantly declined six months after I began this exploration of the vagus nerve. December is the month of Christmas, our wedding anniversary, and my birthday. I realized that I had enjoyed each event of December 2018 more fully than I ever had since losing a daughter in January 2000, followed by the deaths of my parents within fifteen months.

Part of me could say it was because of my continued studies and practices in the areas of mindfulness and their applications to my profession as an SLP. Yet, despite these practices, I still threw my hands to the dashboard of the car when Chuck got too close to another car or braked suddenly. In November 2005, I had been unharmed in an accident that totaled my car. While I was not found to be at fault, some internal voice often warned, "Too close. Watch out." Afterwards the voice complained, "Why does he drive so close to cars?" Such thoughts persisted even though I would remind myself that Chuck is an excellent driver.

I realized these "warnings" quieted significantly when I wore my compression collar. When Chuck mentioned feeling more motivated, I realized all of this in a flash. He may have overcome some internal communication of resistance. Again, my thoughts went back to one of the first videos I had seen on the Q Collar (Washington, n.d.). Washington reported doing a physical mind-challenging task better when she put the collar on. There was nothing more mentioned about this immediate shift in performance. Yet, it is what inspired me to make my own compression collar in order to experience what might happen. It was not until Chuck mentioned feeling more motivated at the gym that I suspected that the innervation of the ventral vagus nerve may quiet those internal communication debates. While they may be well-meaning attempts to "protect" us, they can also challenge trust and hinder progress.

Does "harnessing" the ventral vagus nerve by putting pressure on the neck with a collar, yawning, widening the nostrils, swallowing, and a multitude of other natural gestures and expressions prompt some benevolent, nonjudgmental, quiet telegraphic voice of wisdom? If so, it means that certain behaviors may put a brake on our problem-solving faculties of executive function that are employed to dialogue about the pros and cons of challenging experiences and opportunities. Debates between our inner voices of logic and emotion can go on so long that they can actually hinder forward progress. More pieces of this puzzle began to fit together, and it all made greater sense when I considered the word "survival."

A functional larynx is essential for respiration, swallowing, and speech; yet, it is fragile. The only bone in the laryngeal area is the hyoid bone, which floats in cartilage rather than being connected to another bone. The larynx is primarily composed of hyaline cartilage (epiglottis, thyroid cartilage, cricoid cartilage, arytenoid cartilage, corniculate cartridge, and trachea) connected by ligaments (cricothyroid ligament and vocal cords). Protection of the larynx is crucial for survival. The lateral neck muscles are what primarily offers it protection as well the reflexes of throwing the hands up to the throat, bowing the head to the chest, or shrugging the shoulders. If the throat is attacked or put in a vulnerable situation, defenses must be engaged that simulate a kind of muscular "armor." Then the mind must tap into innate functions of the body to initiate a simple plan for immediate escape. There is no time for the voices of emotion to shout out warnings or the higher cerebral centers to enter into a debate over the situation. There is no time for voices of logic to offer solutions.

Instead, the vagus nerve may be triggered by behaviors that stimulate neurochemicals, such as nitric oxide, to counteract fear. Struggle is inhibited, and a quite benevolent voice of simple and basic reason comes forward and calmly offers a short gentle command. And this internal voice, which is committed to helping us survive and prosper, is heard and obeyed often on a subconscious level even when survival is not immediately threatened. One name for this "voice" is intuition. Intuition is defined as "the ability to perceive or know things without conscious reasoning" (Webster's, 2018:764). Intuition is both innate and developed through episodic memory.

It was in May 2019 when I read Crossman and Neary's (2015:167) discussion of memory from a limbic system perspective. "Memory of events and their past motivations and emotional connotations are the only guide to future complex social behaviour and are also the essential links that preserve the individual in permitting rapid response to potentially threatening situations." They went on to say that the executive functions of the neocortex for critical problem solving could be bypassed in order for the limbic system to generate a survival response. In this way, "highly emotional experiences are readily learned and remembered."

Before reading Crossman and Neary, I had already observed how light touch on the sides of the neck triggers tension in the neck even when the larynx is not physically threatened. This can be sensed unconsciously through proprioception even if the fingertips do not feel the tension on the neck. The Polyvagal Theory calls it neuroception. As I mentioned earlier, touching my neck triggers my nostrils to widen. Consciously widening the nostrils tenses the neck at the area of the omohyoid muscles. With hands trained to palpate, I continued to investigate that area of my neck order to assess what behaviors triggered similar tension. I produced a variety of nonverbal language behaviors (postures, gestures, and facial expressions) and discovered that there were specific behaviors that produced tension in the same location of my neck. These factors expanded my hypothesis about the potential relationship between nonverbal language and ventral vagus nerve toning.

The ability of the limbic system to bypass executive functions combined with the positive mood created by the compression collar, the yawn, widening my nostrils, and touch inspired my next hypothesis. *This is that specific voluntary behaviors could be employed to tone the ventral vagus nerve pathways for enhanced presence of mind and rapport when there is not an immediate threat to survival. These behaviors may actually exercise and strengthen the limbic system's neural pathways in order for the sympathetic nervous system to be less reactive when the heightened stress for immediate survival is not indicated.* The parasympathetic system is triggered to reset.

This is the underlying purpose for establishing rapport—to help clients engage the parasympathetic system of social engagement as quickly as possible. The client, family, and/or caretaker have found themselves to be in challenging circumstances regarding physical, mental, emotional, and/or spiritual health. The therapy process is going to ask all who are involved to master new skills by learning conscientious living. Adapting to health and/or learning-related challenges involves making changes in perceptions, beliefs, feelings, self-esteem, and confidence in order for the individuals to take the personal responsibility necessary to participate in therapy, develop new habits, and use volition optimally.

It makes sense that establishing authentic rapport through ventral vagus nerve activation could reduce tension and enhance interpersonal communication in ways that invites our intuition to respond to change. Volition involves "making choices, self-monitoring, and self-regulation" (Anderson, 1989:413). Making choices involves the ability to imagine outcomes. Nicolosi, et al. (1978:101) define imagination as the "act or ability of forming a mental image of something not present to the senses or never before wholly perceived." Establishing rapport involves the first impressions, "which are critically important in setting the tone for their subsequent interaction. . . . Interpersonal tension is greatest during the initial moments, when people know least what to expect. . . ." (Mortensen, 1972:262-263). Therefore, establishing authentic rapport would have a positive effect on the choices made from the diagnosis, prognosis, goals, treatment plans, and instruction during therapy.

Ventral vagus nerve toning and my improved rapport within myself and with others would explain my greater enjoyment of December 2018 even though I thought I had enjoyed the celebrations years previously. It would explain my improved sense of ease when the grandchildren became boisterous. However, I was still not satisfied that I had gathered enough evidence from the literature to support my findings. The omohyoid muscle was mentioned in the first paragraph of the first article I read in July 2018. I knew one technique well that employed the omohyoid muscle. It is the effortful swallow, which is used in dysphagia therapy. The gulp is also an effortful swallow, so I turned to the researching the swallow, which added the importance of neuroplasticity.

Ten

THE SWALLOW AND NEUROPLASTICITY

"The particular patterns of synaptic connections in an individual's brain, and the information encoded by these connections, are the keys to who the person is."
Joseph LeDoux (2002:3)

Along with breathing, the swallow is an essential survival mechanism. Chapter Eight mentions research showing that the swallow often follows the yawn (Kimiko, et al. 2015) and (Ertekin, et al. 2015). The results confirmed that the yawn involves the lower motor nerves that trigger the swallow as well as being important for the social engagement system: Cranial nerves V, VII, IX, X, XI, and XII. It was stated by the Q Collar developers that light compression on the sides of the neck just above the clavicle does the same thing as the yawn, which occurs due to the pressure innervating the omohyoid muscle (Lemire, 2017). As I mentioned in Chapter One, Dr. David Smith, M.D. said that when the omohyoid activates, it "pulls straight back and collapses the jugular vein. This happens each and every time you yawn."

The omohyoid is one of four muscles belonging to the infrahyoid muscle group. The infrahyoid muscles run below the hyoid bone and to the larynx and thorax. They are important for the end stage of the swallow. The primary action is to lower both the hyoid bone and the larynx to their original positions after the swallow. They are innervated by the hypoglossal cranial nerve (CN XII).

The omohyoid is a two-directional muscle with a fairly fixed central tendon. On each side of the neck, it goes from the scapula in the shoulder to the hyoid bone. From the scapula, it is a flat "narrow band across the lower part of the neck, passing behind the sternocleidomastoid muscle" (Palmer, 1972:108). From there it attaches to the clavicle in the form of a tendon. Then it rises vertically and, paralleling the sternohyoid muscle, attaches to the lower body of the hyoid bone just lateral to the sternohyoid. It depresses, retracts, and pulls the hyoid bone to one side or the other. "It is also believed that the omohyoids contract during deep inspiration to stiffen the neck blood vessels during the inspiratory action" (Palmer, 1972:108). The omohyoid not only produces the end stage of the swallow, it also lowers the larynx in order to shorten the vocal cords for vocalizing low pitches and low vowels.

Researchers Moisik and Gick (2017) analyzed the larynx from the perspective of quantal biomechanics and used computer models. "Quantality is one property that can help increase the controllability of body structures given realistic limitation of the capacity of the central nervous system." Neuroscience has long recognized that the central nervous system is finite even though the motor system has seemingly infinite freedom in movements. Research continues to support the concept that the nervous system "has a 'library' of neuromuscular modules, each built with a specific function" (Moisik and Gick, 2017:540). Here again, I had not found anything that conflicted with what I observed about triggering the ventral vagus nerve through nonverbal language movements such as grasping the neck and widening the nostrils. Quantality is a concept that could actually explain how certain behaviors trigger the autonomic nervous system to return to a state of homeostasis. A well recognized strategy for countering stress is conscious breathing.

Moisik and Gick (2017:546) identify inspiration to be an "integral component of the sequence of motor behaviors characterizing speech." The coordination of the swallow with the breath is also essential for safe deglutition (swallowing). Just as Moisik and Gick report inspiration to precede and follow vocalizations, inspiration precedes and follows the swallow. During the inspiration phase, the larynx lowers and the tongue base (genioglossus muscle) moves forward. This is most evident during deep inspiration. The distance between the hyoid bone and thyroid cartilage (hyolaryngeal excursion) widens causing the soft tissue in the larynx to move vertically, which optimizes airflow by lowering resistance. The sternohyoid is anterior to the omohyoid, and it also lowers the larynx. I touched my neck and discovered that deep inspiration occurred with greater ease. My nostrils also widened. A sigh followed. What happens when you touch your neck and inhale?

One dysphagia therapy intervention is to activate sensory pathways. This is accomplished through touch, temperature, taste, and electrical stimulation. The goal is to help trigger the sequence of motor behaviors of the swallow after the activation of afferent (sensory) neural pathways. Performing any action (including thought) is to exercise the nerves that activate the movements. Therefore, innervating nerves means to exercise them. An important goal in dysphagia, voice, and articulation therapy involves improving the coordination of breath support (inhalation and exhalation) with the swallow, phonation (voice), and speech sound production. A full return of function means the nerves have healed. Improvements in function mean that new pathways have grown through learning. This is called neuroplasticity or neural plasticity. I returned to researching ASHA's publications for research on the nervous system of the swallow, especially "neuroplasticity."

Researchers Robbins et al. (2008:S208) defined neuroplasticity and offered recommendations for a collaborative approach between "clinical and basic scientists" regarding "potential research direction in dysphagia" particularly in respect to "neural plasticity." They acknowledged that clinical evidence gathered by the practitioners often "outpaced science and evidence to support them." Neural plasticity refers to the brain's ability to change. Central nervous system plasticity refers to changes in physiological/behavioral function as a result of changes arising from personal experience with one's environment, training, and physiology from aging to disease. Neural plasticity involves a "change in synaptic function within a particular central neural substrate" (Robbins et al., 2008:S277). These researches made an important distinction within behavioral changes. "Although neural plasticity may result in a behavioral change, not all behavioral change necessarily involves neural plasticity." Some changes involve compensation, which means different neural substrates were engaged to achieve a desired outcome.

This differentiation relates to what I had observed evolving from using my compression collar and then doing specific behaviors that created similar tension in the neck as well. They all promoted an uplifted feeling. As I had mentioned in Chapter Five, Coleman and Davidson (2017) identified changes that are constant and enduring to be new traits learned though experience. These shape the brain through a neurological process that we are unaware of. This fit with my observation that while I was able to tone down my reactions to negative feelings by using techniques that promoted presence of mind, my blood pressure readings at the medical office showed that something had not changed on a synaptic level. I may have learned to adjust to a rise in blood pressure by activating the nonverbal behaviors that reflect states of calmness even though I was stressed. This suggests that I may have been compensating by acting calm even though my heart may have been overexerting itself. Certain nonverbal language behaviors (pragmatics), such as slower relaxed speech, using inflections, and a smile, may have caused me to believe that I was relaxed even though I wasn't.

According to neuroscientist Joseph LeDoux (2002), the self as personality is determined, at least in part, by a neural process. "The particular patterns of synaptic connections in an individual's brain, and the information encoded by these connections, are the keys to who the person is." Most of these systems are plastic, meaning that synapses are changed by experience. Synapses are the connections between neurons, and "they are the main channels of information flow and storage in the brain" (LeDoux, 2002:2-3).

"Synaptic connections are adjusted by environmentally driven neural activity in specific neural systems" (LeDoux, 2002:306). According to LeDoux, the processing occurs "in parallel" among a variety of the senses, and modulators assist in the coordination. Modulators serve to regulate neurotransmissions at the synapses that are already active and process information about an experience. One class of modulators is monoamines. They are in the brainstem, but have axons widespread throughout the brain. These include substances like serotonin, dopamine, epinephrine, and norepinephrine, which can influence cells in various locations. Therefore, they are "not involved in precise representation of stimuli in specific circuits . . . but produce global state changes in many brain areas simultaneously, from a high degree of arousal . . . to going to sleep" (LeDoux, 2002:58).

LeDoux (2002:307) does not see any difference between developmental plasticity (which occurs early in life) and learning (which occurs lifelong). I could not find anything in LeDoux's observations that negated what I was experiencing by placing my fingers on the sides of my neck. Instead, I could now say that it is a global sensation of wellbeing that occurs along a continuum of awareness. It occurred when high alertness was required as well as when I was ready to sleep. I could now consider the likelihood that certain behaviors trigger these modulators, which could actually be trained throughout one's lifetime. This inspired me to continue exploring research on neuroplasticity in order to explore the clinical possibilities. One area of research is rehabilitation in general. In the field of speech-language pathology, the treatment of the swallow fits well with neuroplasticity.

An abstract of an article written by Ruth E. Martin (2009) states that there has been a surge of research on neuroplasticity beginning in the early 1990's. Yet, its importance was identified in the 1960's from enrichment studies with animals, particularly rats. Rats raised in an enriched environment had larger brains whether the enrichment occurred developmentally or in adulthood. Now, neuroscience has shown that neuroplastic changes can be associated with behavioral alteration, which result from experiences that effect brain morphology and/or function.

According to Ianessa Humbert, neuroplasticity has become "a new paradigm for the development of rehabilitative strategies," and dysphagia therapies have the capacity to improve neuroplasticity (Humbert, 2011:11-13). Now, not only motor control, but also the sensory component of action (sensory integration) is an important part of neuroscience research. The oral, pharyngeal, and laryngeal structures involve a sensory system that is extremely diverse and rich compared to the rest of the body. These three structures (including the tongue's taste buds) have mucous membrane epithelial linings, which "offer a vast array of sensory modalities" that a bite of food or sip of liquid will stimulate. (Humbert, 2011:11).

These sensations, which include "general sensation (touch/pressure)," taste, texture, temperature, and the sense of smell, are modalities that stimulate these systems as well. I suggest the reader review Hubert's article for greater details of sensory integration. I took particular interest in the identification of general sensation from touch and pressure. That is what I have been applying when using the compression collar and by touching my throat.

In regard to movement, Humbert (2011:12) writes, "Effortless movement occurs when continuous sensory information is processed continually before, during, and after a movement." This involves "planning, executing, and evaluating an action." Humbert went on to differentiate between reflexes and voluntary movements, the general consensus being that reflexes require "a trigger, are difficult to suppress once in motion, and are controlled by lower brain areas" (brainstem or spinal cord). The swallow is both reflexive and voluntary. Few would argue that the yawn is also both, as well as nonverbal language behaviors.

While science may debate where a behavior is reflexive verses behavioral, some are considering it to be a continuum between what is a reflexive and what is under voluntary control. Humbert pointed out that the Mendelsohn maneuver, which is used by SLPs in dysphagia therapy, actually disrupts the triggered swallow at the pharyngeal phase by "prolonging hyo-laryngeal movement" through voluntary (higher cortical) actions. Humbert offered the important point that "endogenous," "intention-based" or "top-down," are tactics whereby the client produces movements or pays attention to the sensations according to the instructions of the clinician.

The Mendelsohn maneuver was important to consider because it postpones the hyo-laryngeal lowering action of the omohyoid muscles. I engaged in an experiment while doing this maneuver. Holding the larynx up voluntarily requires greater tongue pressure against the nasal pharynx. This prevents inspiration. Doing the maneuver created the opposite of elevated mood. Instead, I found that the overall sensation fit best with immobility, which is the sympathetic state triggered by the dorsal vagus nerve. What do you feel when you try it?

I repeated the Mendelsohn maneuver multiple times, and each time my head and neck moved back slightly as if withdrawing. Adding the tactile pressure on my neck did not produce that familiar elevated mood nor did it reduce the tension being created by the Mendelsohn maneuver. Also, I was unable to widen my nostrils. I realized that this maneuver had the opposite effect of those nonverbal behaviors that I believe activate the ventral vagus nerve. Importantly, I could only relate it to being a highly exaggerated form of hacking in order to clear phlegm. It is not a nonverbal language behavior that falls within pragmatics.

The Mendelsohn maneuver is also unnatural. It is a much more exaggerated motor behavior. Clients have to be trained to do it in order to compensate for and strengthen a weak swallow. The instruction and practice results in improved motor control of the technique; therefore, neuroplasticity occurs.

Neurobiology research is confirming that there must be sufficient change in the nervous system for new learning to occur. Neuroscience has shown that "neural plasticity is the mechanism by which the brain encodes experience and learns new behaviors" (Kleim and Jones, 2008: S225, S226). This is "experience-dependent neural neuroplasticity." The researchers identified ten principals of experience-dependent plasticity that can influence plasticity in both intact and damaged brains. I direct the reader back to this article for the full content. Functions must be used to improve them and in order not to lose them. Sufficient repetition and intensity of exertion is important. The content must have "saliency" in order for learners to have a sense that the material is important.

Neuroplasticity can carry over to the development of desired skills and help to prevent the development or continuation of unwanted behaviors. I realized that experience-dependent neural plasticity learning principals fit well with integrating nonverbal language exercises early into therapy to activate the ventral vagus nerve functions for authentic rapport. Also, each discovery was supporting my suspicions that something very important was developing regarding learning as well.

It is widely accepted that experience precedes learning. Research has shown that enriched environments promote better health. "People who experience warmer, more upbeat emotions live longer and healthier lives" (Kok et. al, 2012: 1122). For decades, health research regarding the correlations between positive emotions, better health, and longevity continues to build a strong case that positivity promotes healthiness. Kok et al.'s research looked at what happens to physical health when emotions are manipulated. They used cardiac vagal tone as the objective indicator of health. They based this indicator on Porges's (2007) findings regarding heart rate variability (HRV). Porges sites the 1915 book by Eppinger and Hess, which shows that for over a century, variations in the tone of the vagus nerve system has been attributed to health problems such as respiratory arrhythmia and habitual bradycardia (abnormally slow heart rate). More follows on this in Chapter Eleven.

Two medical diagnoses that are often found in the medical history of patients with aspiration pneumonia due to dysphagia are cardiomyopathy and chronic pulmonary obstruction disease. This was on my mind when I read an article by Ertekin and Aydogdu (2003:2226). The swallow is "a complex sensorimotor behavior involving the coordinated contraction and inhibition of the musculature located around the mouth, at the tongue, larynx, pharynx and esophagus bilaterally."

This "behavior" is divided into three phases, which are related to the process of how the swallow is innervated. The oral phase by voluntary muscles, the pharyngeal phase being a reflex, and the esophageal phase being controlled by the somatic and autonomic nervous system. The researchers' focus was on the oral and pharyngeal phase of the swallow.

The sensory and motor fibers that trigger the swallow involve the trigeminal nerve (CNV), the glossopharyngeal nerve (CNIX), and the superior laryngeal branch of the vagus nerve (CNX). These cranial nerves "are excited and/or inhibited sequentially for the execution of the passage of the bolus from the mouth to the stomach" (Ertekin and Aydogdu, 2003:2226). I suggest that clinicians who are interested in the rich details regarding the swallow review this article. According to these researchers, the oral cavity and pharynx are highly integrated regions of the head and neck. They have an essential involvement and "intimate interrelationship" in the motor behaviors required for successful "feeding, chewing, swallowing, speech, and respiration" (Ertekin and Aydogdu, 2003:2228). The suprahyoid muscles contract during the pharyngeal phase to elevate the hyoid bone and larynx. This enables the vocal cords to abduct firmly in order to protect the airway from the bolus that is passing through the pharynx. This happens in "both voluntarily initiated and spontaneous reflex swallows" (Ertekin and Aydogdu, 2003:2232).

While it has been held that the pharyngeal swallow is mediated principally by brainstem mechanisms, "electrophysiological, neuroimaging, and clinical studies indicate that the cerebral cortex plays a fundamental role in the regulation of the swallowing (Ertekin and Aydogdu, 2003: 3326.) Knowing the involvement of the vagus nerve with the heart, respiration, and relaxation, I began to wonder what role the omohyoid muscles of the infrahyoid group might have in regard to the esophageal phase of the swallow. Yet, that investigation would sidetrack me from the goal of this guidebook. The laryngeal anatomy and physiology for voice and the swallow are involved and complicated, inspiring endless avenues for research in regard to ventral vagus nerve involvement.

This guidebook does not even touch upon the anatomy and physiology of facial expressions except for identifying the cranial nerves. What is most important and salient is that nonverbal language exercises and gentle tactile stimulation of the neck and larynx do no harm. Instead, based on research of the swallow, the exercises actually can tone the vagus nerve through neuroplasticity in ways that facilitates function and, very likely, learning.

For the sake of providing sufficient evidence, I have researched multiple articles and obtained books regarding what the ventral vagus nerve can do and by what means. Yet for me, every answer provoked another question, which offered many directions of exploration including phenomenology, the science of touch, embodied self-awareness, sensory integration, interception, exteroception, the swallow, the yawn, and pragmatics. I have come to "see" this area of exploration metaphorically. It is like the discovery of a longstanding underground river that has many steams branching off and smaller springs that rise above ground. For me, the vagus nerve (and Polyvagal Theory) is that river, and compression of the neck is a stream.

The intention behind my literature research and informal studies since July 2018 has been to understand how is it that a compression collar putting pressure on the sides of the neck can enhance overall functioning. My conclusion is that *it stimulates the ventral vagus nerve system (which involves other cranial nerves) in a manner that heightens rapport and even promotes health, wellness, and supports success with daily activities of life.* Yet, that seems more like an underground stream rather than a spring percolating visibly. It is the spring that I have been searching for.

In regard to the sympathetic and parasympathetic nervous system, Eppinger and Hess (1915:18) noted: "Hence it may be stated that the normal progress of functioning of visceral organs is a well regulated interaction between two contrary acting forces." The authors' diagram of this interaction is like a teeter-totter. When the amygdala stimulates adrenalin, the activation of the sympathetic nervous system rises. The parasympathetic system goes down. On the other end, "if a weight be taken from" the parasympathetic nervous system, it rises. Adrenalin and the responses of the sympathetic system go down. This would be what Porges refers to as the vagus brake, which reduces adrenalin and allows the ventral vagus system to rise up and return the system to homeostasis.

Porges (2017:125) stresses that exercises need to be developed that "recruit these neural circuits that support health, growth, and restoration." This recruiting would lower the adrenalin-stimulated sympathetic nervous system and allow the parasympathetic nervous system to activate. However, within all my research, I did not find suggestions on how to recruit these neural circuits directly through natural behaviors like touch or nonverbal language movements. Most of the suggestions are more indirect activities like meditation, exercise, and breath work. Newberg and Waldman (2010) did identify one natural behavior that directly recruits the parasympathetic nervous system—the yawn. The yawn has been shown to create that state of homeostasis. Homeostasis happens when there are well-regulated interactions within the autonomic nervous system.

At first, very few publications in ASHA's professional literature came up when searching "vagus nerve." I suspected that one reason for the absence of research is that speech-language pathology services are directed towards achieving the highest level of functional communication and/or swallow outcomes. Documentation addresses muscular rather than neural-network stimulation techniques even though the functional outcomes are actually produced by improving these neural networks. Also, the concerns and insights of patients and families regarding impaired communication and swallowing difficulties are generally addressed through "counseling."

However, establishing authentic rapport to enhance the focusing skills necessary for optimum learning, growth and/or restoration through direct physical stimulation or engaging in movements that stimulate the vagus nerve is not a paradigm shift for speech-language pathologists or audiologists. This is because many of the therapy techniques employed and the developmental or adaptive skills that we teach actually appear to be improving the tone of the ventral vagus nerve even though not identified as a goal. Yet, when I added the word "assessment" and then "heart rate variability" to "vagus nerve" more articles on the vagus nerve became available when searching for ASHA's publications. I turned to researching ways that the ventral vagus nerve can be assessed.

Eleven

ASSESSING AND INNERVATING THE VAGUS NERVE

"Most of them are sudden—head and body jerks, foot or head movements, inhalations, facial grimaces, nasal snorts."   Charles Van Riper (1971:134)

Before therapeutic strategies are initiated to improve a skill, an assessment is made of the current status in order to determine the therapy pathway and evaluate progress. I wondered what might be available to use as an objective indicator (rather than subjective provider/client reporting) of improved attention from vagal pathways strengthening. Optimal attention is a reason for establishing rapport. Switching to researching ways to assess the vagus nerve led to an ASHA publication (Watson, 2010) about its relationship to autism spectrum disorder (ASD). It not only supported what I have been observing, it also showed that the Polyvagal Theory has already been incorporated into the field of speech-language pathology. An excellent review of this theory is provided in this article (Watson, 2010:1054).

Watson et al. (2010) did a longitudinal study that investigated the correlation of child-directed speech (CDS) to the functional communication skills of children with ASD. One role of CDS is that it appears to enhance children's language learning. Another concept for CDS that most people are familiar with is baby talk. The study involved assessing behavioral and physiological responses as predictors of their language and social skills. The primary physiological response was "vagal activity as physiological indices of attention quality, and the vagal system in children with ASD" (Watson et al., 2010:1053). Watson et al. describe CDS to have "higher pitch, greater pitch range, less diversity in vocabulary, and more references to the here and now." This article states that research has shown that children from age one month to preschool years attend better to CDS rather than adult-directed speaking styles.

Attention involves involuntary and voluntary components of behavior (Watson, 2010:1053). "Orienting" is primary. It involves an "involuntary, reactive phase of attention that occurs immediately following the onset of a novel stimulus." Sustained attention is more voluntary, and maintaining attention to CDS in early

65

childhood is assumed to be essential for learning effective social-communication skills. "Attention skills, like all behaviors, have underlying physiological bases that can be measured and examined for variability." Voluntarily focusing on a stimulus involves behaviors that "are associated with physiological changes, such as slowing of the heart rate." These changes are mediated by the parasympathetic nervous system and are associated with the "rest/digest" function of the vagus nerve system.

A measure of vagal activity involves heart rate variability because of the role of the vagus nerve in regulating the heartbeat. "In a resting state, heart rate varies depending on the phase of the respiratory cycle, with an increase in heart rate on inspiration and a decrease in rate on expiration" (Watson, 2010: 1054). This is called respiratory sinus arrhythmia (RSA), and it is an index of vagal activation. It involves the difference between rates that are indicating the amount of vagal influence. The greater the RSA variation is, the greater the vagal activity.

Research has shown a higher RSA in infants who cried when mildly frustrated correlates positively to the ability to adapt over time. "Among preschoolers, higher resting RSA is related to higher concurrent social competence, better emotional regulation, and lower levels of problem behavior. . . . In general, the higher resting RSA is associated with more positive development and social-emotional outcomes" (Watson, 2010: 1054). Studies have shown that the levels and changes in RSA decrease "in response to negative social stressors and increase in response to positive social interactions." The research concluded that there is a possibility that "children with ASD might benefit from interventions that stimulate the vagus" (Watson, 2010:1062). I palpated my neck while doing CDS and felt that familiar tension. I felt the omohyoid muscles tense. CDS was activating the vagus nerve.

It is widely accepted that experience precedes learning. Research has shown that enriched environments promote better health. "People who experience warmer, more upbeat emotions live longer and healthier lives" (Kok et. al, 2012: 1122). For decades health research regarding the correlations between positive emotions, better health, and longevity continues to build a strong case that positivity promotes healthiness. Kok et al.'s research looked at what happens to physical health when emotions are manipulated positively. The objective indicator of health that they used was cardiac vagal tone. They based this indicator on Porges's (2007) findings regarding heart rate variability (HRV), which I mentioned in Chapter Ten.

The book by Eppinger and Hess that Porges (2017) referenced is *Vagotonia: A Clinical Study in Vegetative Neurology* (1915). That means variations in the tone of the vagus nerve system has been attributed to health problems such as respiratory arrhythmia and habitual bradycardia for over a century. "There is no doubt, owing to its close relations to the glands of internal secretion, the autonomic nervous system [extended vagus nerve] has a marked influence . . . upon the entire mechanism of metabolism" (Eppinger and Hess, 1915:17).

Although I first accessed a public domain version of Eppinger and Hess's book, the content was important enough to order a reprint. While its focus is pharmaceutical, the authors were searching for clues that related the health of nerves to "nervous disorders." They were specifically looking at the tone of the vagus nerve, and too much tone is identified as "vagotonia." Eppinger and Hess (1915:2) defined the "animal" nervous system as being the sensorimotor system that is used "at will." The "vegetative" nervous system involves the "fibers" that go to organs, smooth muscles (blood vessels, gland ducts, and skin) as well as the "fibers that influence secretory functions upon glands." Vegetative fibers also include the cross-striated muscles of organs from the heart to the muscles of the "genital apparatus." All of these muscles function similarly to smooth muscles except for the heart.

Three branches were identified: midbrain, bulbar, and sacral. Midbrain fibers "subserve" the functions of the eyes. The bulbar segment proceeds in part by way of the facial and glossopharyngeal nerves to supply fibers to the glands and vasodilators of the head. "The largest and most important of this segment [midbrain] is the vagus, the principal nerve of the viscera" (Eppinger and Hess, 1915:4). The sacral segment involves the pelvic nerves, which supply the descending colon, the sigmoid, anus, bladder, and "genital apparatus."

In 1915, it was "customary" to identify "all nerves [that] arose from the sympathetic cord as 'sympathetic,' while all other vegetative nerves of the nervous system are spoken of as the "autonomic [the system of the extended vagus]" (Eppinger and Hess, 1915:4). The different nerves within the two systems may be "commingled on their way to the end organs making anatomical differentiation impossible and physiological testing difficult." One thing that was very important to me was their observation that the pelvic nerves go beyond the intestines and down to the "genital apparatus," yet there is commingling as "the system of the extended vagus nerve." The best Internet image I have found of this commingling is by Georgia Highland College in an Internet "Vox" article by Stromberg (2015).

This concept of commingling fits with another observation I had made while exploring natural behaviors that generated similar omohyoid muscle tension as the yawn. A surprising activity was doing kegels (the tightening of muscles that stop the flow of urine). I had wondered if my imagination was going too far. My discovery of what Eppinger and Hess identified as the extended vagus and the concept of commingling inspired me to research the vagus nerve, uterus, and cervix. The vagus nerve does serve to connect the uterus and cervix with the central nervous system (Collins, J.J., et al., 1999). Vaginal and clitoral sexual arousal are conveyed in the pudendal, hypogastric, pelvic, and vagus nerves (Giuliano, F., et al., 2002). Following spinal cord injury, a significant number of males achieve erections and ejaculate during intercourse (Loler J.M., et al., 2018). While this guidebook cannot go into the role of the vagus nerve in sexuality, it does support the idea that doing kegels can stimulate the vagus nerve. One must remain calm in order to find a restroom.

I needed to leave internal exercises of the sacral organs to another area of research for the future. For now, my focus needed be on the heart and how it can be used to assess the tone of the vagus nerve. According to Porges (2007), researchers once believed that a healthy heart had a stable rhythm. Any variations were attributed to the research conditions. Some psychological reactivity to the stimulus was affecting heart rate. However, when equipment became sophisticated enough to measure heartbeat changes accurately, understanding HRV required a shift in the theoretical orientation of the cardiovascular system.

In the early 1990's, the shift began to turn away from the stimulus-response theory that considered heart rate patterns to be responsive behaviors. Instead, there was a growing appreciation that there were complex neuromechanisms mediating heart rate changes. Rather than heart beat patterns being a response to stimuli, HRV views it as a "system" model that "incorporated an elaboration of feedback mechanisms from the periphery and central modulators of the output gain of efferent pathways" (Porges, 2007:119). The feedback mechanism depends on the visceral afferent pathways and "central regulatory features" such as the medulla and hypothalamus, which "interpret the afferent feedback and exert control over the motor output back to the visceral organs."

Heart rate variability (HRV) has even become an indicator in speech, language, and hearing research. A recent study (Seeman and Sims, 2015) looked at HRV as a measurement of listening effort. They reported that HRV is being used in cardiology and psychology to measure stress response. While there are a wide variety of "physiological indicators" to measure listening effort and increased mental demands (pupil dilation, skin conductance, and electromyogenic responses), HRV is now being used to study listening effort.

The theory is that decreased HRV occurs with higher physical and mental demands as well as when there is abnormal autonomic nervous-system function. "When stress is increased, sympathetic nervous-system activity is higher, resulting in increased HR [heart rate] and a decreased HRV. On the contrary, when stress is low, the parasympathetic nervous system dominates. During these periods of low stress or rest, parasympathetic (vagal) inputs from stress receptors in the lungs and vascular system cause HR to vary widely (i.e. respiratory sinus arrhythmia), increasing and decreasing HR synchronously with the breathing cycle" (Seeman and Sims, 2015:1782). In their study, HRV showed greater sensitivity to task complexity than did skin conductance.

In regard to HRV and aphasia (Christensen and Wright, 2014:S362), past research has suggested that language performance by individuals with aphasia is affected by effort allocated. If this is true, the authors hypothesize that "it may be possible to instruct individuals with aphasia to appropriately pre-evaluate the task difficulty and to match the effort they invest with the task demands." Yet, before this study, measurements of effort and task difficulty for individuals with aphasia have been subjective reporting by the clinician and client. Christensen and Wright (2014:S369) identify multiple studies that show that the cardiovascular system responds to changes in effort applied to tasks that vary in difficulty. This offers "the potential to provide insight into the effort individuals with aphasia allocate to verbal and nonverbal tasks. A well-studied measure of effort allocated to cognitively demanding tasks is heart rate variability (HRV)." The "heart rate responds quickly to changes in workload, so the measure is appropriate for . . . studies of short duration." One of the results of the study was that individuals with aphasia had impaired physiological response to tasks that increased in difficulty. The authors also concluded that both physiological measures and "subjective self-reporting" measures combined have value.

Further investigation into HRV led to a surprising research article from 1936: "A Study of the Heart Rate During Stuttering" (Travis et al., 1936). The authors recorded heart potentials from electrocardiograms and respiratory cycles from a pheumograph on film while control group and individuals who stutter were silent or did oral reading. They reported even then that "under certain conditions in man, inspiration is accompanied by acceleration, and expiration by a retardation of heart rate has been observed by us in this present study" (Travis et al., 1936:22). They also found that the "mean" expiratory heart rate slowed even more during speaking, "probably due to a more forcibly and blocked expiration than during silence." However, "when inspiration and expiration were considered together, the heart beat was faster during speech than during silence for both groups of subjects" most likely due to the increased activity.

Being before HRV, these authors were looking more directly at the heart rate itself. They discovered that "the stutter's heart rate was faster than 'normals' for both inspiration and expiration during both silence and speaking" (Travis et al., 1936:23). They attributed this to increased emotionality. Also, the authors describe "interesting phenomena" in stuttering. One was the Valsalva effect during a "spasm" whereby the heart rate became slower. Tremors were also noted in the breathing mechanism (ten per second) as well as other "breathing abnormalities during stuttering." These included "prolonged inspiration, interruption of expiration by short inspiratory movements, failure of the breathing mechanism to move either in or out, and attempts on the stutter to speak on relatively empty lungs." A few showed premature ventricular contractions and some showed excessive general muscular tension while speaking. Travis et al. concluded that the changes in heart rate during speech in both groups were due to changes in breathing and "general bodily activity."

Travis et al. (1936) provided me with an entirely different perspective regarding secondary characteristics displayed by many who stutter. Along with doing research of the literature, I was generating a list of nonverbal language behaviors that resulted in similar tension of the omohyoid muscles. After reading the article by Travis et al., I realized that the observed "phenomena" was similar to the behaviors used to move out of a block and back into fluency. According to Van Riper (1971:134) these are called "interruptor devices," which are "escape behaviors" that can range from being minimally noticeable to the "bizarre" in those with severe stuttering. "Most of them are sudden—head and body jerks, foot or head movements, inhalations, facial grimaces, nasal snorts." Van Riper distinguishes between interruptor devices and avoidances. Avoidances are those tactics and strategies cognitively devised to avoid circumstances where stuttering might occur. According to Van Riper, interruptor devices can be extinguished easier than avoidance responses.

From a ventral vagus nerve perspective, I could now consider the interruptor behaviors to be compensatory strategies that trigger the vagus nerve braking system just enough to enhance the outcome of the specific utterance. However, they do not result in changes of the synapses that promote natural fluency nor do those behaviors become set motor adaptations because they are extinguishable. What I found to be very motivating is that many of these interruptors are behaviors that I had identified as nonverbal language behaviors that stimulate the vagus nerve— grasping the throat, grimacing, sniffing, shrugging the shoulders, verbal interjections such as "uh," etc. The vagus nerve, being twenty percent motor, is also involved in innervating important motor systems for verbal expression. I realized it was now time to investigate and determine the specific nonverbal behaviors that indicate intact vagus nerve functions as well as stimulate the ventral vagus nerve pathways similar to placing fingers on the sides of the neck, yawning, and widening the nostrils. Looking at HRV is the most objectively scientific, but the literature confirmed the subjective process of observation is acceptable as well.

Rosenberg (2017) states that a way to test vagus nerve function is the gag reflex. The gag reflex is a motor function that SLPs trigger in order to assess the palatopharyngeal valve innervated by the vagus nerve. The gag is produced when the pharyngeal branch of the vagus nerve contracts to prevent an unsafe or unwanted bolus (food) from moving beyond the soft palate and below the base of the tongue. Damage to the vagus nerve can result in palatopharyngeal incompetence, thus impairing the gag reflex. Also, Darley et al. (1975:112, 116) discusses impaired voice quality to be related to vagus nerve damage. "Since the vagus nerve and the nucleus ambiguus from which its motor fibers arise are small structures, unilateral lesion of cranial nerve X ordinarily result in weakness of the palate, pharynx, and as well as the vocal fold."

The main difference with Rosenberg's assessment is that he was testing the gag reflex as in indication of vagus nerve tone rather than assessing for vagus nerve intactness. It made sense that a strong voice with good pitch range would be a good indicator of vagus nerve tone as well. I said, "Hello," aloud using a sliding range of pitch from low to high. Then, I placed my fingers on the sides of my neck and voiced, "Hello," attempting the same sliding range of low to high pitch range. I investigated the comparisons ten times; each time, voice quality and range was better when I touched my neck. Interruptor devices took on an entirely new meaning. Yet, not only did certain nonverbal gestures and expressions interrupt a problematic motor response, they actually appeared to be augmentative in regard to enhancing pitch and quality. What happens when you press on your neck and vary *hello*?

As I stressed in Chapter One, it was because of my immediate positive experiences with a compression collar and then by simply putting pressure on the sides of the neck that motivated me to begin this journey of research and exploration. My observations continue to support my hypothesis *that certain motor behaviors have the innate capacity to improve mood and engagement; and therefore, rapport.* Voice quality and pitch range impact rapport. I still had not found anything in the literature or subjective experimentation that negated this. In order to determine what other behaviors could be used to assess the vagus nerve, I needed to determine the ones that, very likely, activated it.

I began to explore the nonverbal motor behaviors that fall under the category of pragmatics. Ironically, my focus was not on the nonverbal actions that communicate positive emotions regarding sociability. Instead, it was on those behaviors that are perceived to express negative emotions. I had begun to hypothesize that *the behaviors perceived to be "negative" might actually activate the ventral vagus nerve pathways.* Tremors in breathing, ventricular contractions, speaking without air, and even the Valsalva maneuver are forms of nonverbal behaviors that may do more than reveal stress and uncomfortable feelings. *They may actually serve to decrease stress by activating the vagus nerve's vagal brake, which returns the system to some degree of homeostasis.* I already had the Valsalva maneuver on my list of actions.

Rosenberg (2015) provided general motor exercises that stimulate the ventral vagus nerve for social engagement. I mentioned that one exercise is to lie on the floor and, without moving the head, look far to the right until a yawn or sigh is emitted. Then repeat the exercise, looking far to the left. Once mastered, the exercise can be done while sitting in a chair. What I knew by now was that the yawn and eye gaze serve to enhance attention for social engagement. A relaxed but direct gaze produces similar tension in the neck and supports interpersonal communication.

"By the glance which reveals the other, one discloses himself. . . . The eye cannot take unless at the same time it gives. What occurs in this direct mutual glance represents the most wonderful reciprocity in the entire field of human relationship"

(Harper, et. al, 1978:171). Early research on the direction of eye gaze found that "reflective questions" caused individuals to move their eyes either to the left or right (Harper, et al., 1978:226). It appears that Rosenberg was teaching an exaggerated form of a natural nonverbal behavior that activates the ventral vagus nerve.

It is very common for SLPs to devise therapy materials for individual clients that are based on evidence. When a technique is consistently successful based on the clinician's objective observation and the client's subjective self-reporting, it becomes an evidence-based practice that can be used with others. Formal objective scientific research often follows. Therefore, my training as an SLP motivated me to investigate innate nonverbal language movements and postures that produced similar omohyoid muscle responses in my neck as well as positive mood. Knowing the vagus nerve's relationship to other cranial nerves, these actions also needed to be related to the functions of cranial nerves V, VII, IX, X, XI and even XII.

I assessed each nonverbal behavior multiple times while gently palpating my neck and focusing on inner sensations (physiological feelings). Then I generated a list of these nonverbal actions from gross motor to fine motor behaviors (from posture to speech sounds) that, very likely, stimulated the ventral vagus nerve at the very least. From there, I investigated behaviors that produced similar sensations, theorizing that touch triggers the ventral vagus nerve. Finally, knowing about the use of imagery in sports medicine and medicine in general, and applying what I had discovered about the precuneus, it was evident that our thoughts (imagination) affect rapport as well. With this in mind, I decided to add metaphors and idioms that may activate the ventral vagus nerve network through the imagination.

I began employing these techniques whenever I felt anxious and observed the results. Each behavior helped me feel more comfortable and in better control of the situation. What I noticed is that my grandchildren's arguments were no longer making me feel anxious. Previously, I would demand that they stop and then approach their disagreements from a cognitive perspective by attempting to engage their executive thinking for problem solving and behavior regulation. Yet not long afterwards, the dispute would continue because the energy from the resentment over some aggressive touch or slight in fairness had not been reversed. But that has changed.

Now, when an argument begins to escalate, I tell them to sit side-by-side rather than attempting to help them rectify their differences. Instead of engaging in verbal reasoning, I have them engage in nonverbal behaviors that I believe stimulate the ventral vagus nerve. I then wait for the result. Consistently, they begin to laugh and even nudge each other affectionately in less than a minute. Roughhousing may resume but it is with laughter instead of angry shouting.

The ventral vagus nerve has activated the body's natural system for homeostasis and social engagement, which is confirmed by their fast return to positive play. I realized that engaging in verbal reasoning when in an angered state could actually backfire and be perceived as some form of punishment. This could cause disengagement from the act of listening. Directing my grandchildren to participate in a nonverbal activity that activates the vagus nerve took away perceptions that punitive repercussions were taking place. Instead, these behaviors promote positive social engagement fairly quickly. I have found that intervention by an "authority" is often unnecessary after the tensions are diffused by vagus nerve activation.

It is important for both the clinician and the client to understand that a number of these nonverbal behaviors and postures have negative social connotations. The yawn is considered to be disrespectful in many cultures. Shrugging shoulders or slumping the shoulders and bowing the head forward can indicate disengagement. Wincing and wailing are more extreme behaviors that indicate distress. Because of the natural socially innate tendency of humans to empathize with others, these behaviors can cause "listeners" who initially feel good actually feel worse. That may be one reason that we often respond to such behaviors with, "Don't do that."

Since he began to walk, one of my grandsons has slumped his shoulders and bowed his head when something did not go the way he desired. Often tears would follow. By the time he was two, the adults began telling him not to respond that way. Even I would try to explain to him why he did not need to "make such a bit deal" about the minor disappointment. Yet, this body language continued into first grade, which was the year I was studying the vagus nerve. I began to suspect that he was engaging a natural posture that served to recruit the ventral vagus nerve and return him to a state of homeostasis. I did not tell him this until I saw basketball star Kevin Durant (K.D.) do the same thing after missing a basket while playing for the Golden State Warriors. Chuck yelled out, "You cannot do that on the court!" I told my grandson that K.D. was innervating his vagus nerve. He smiled with delight, slapped his leg, and then sighed deeply. Now, when he slumps like that, I say, "Hey, you are stimulating your vagus nerve. You will feel better soon." I observed that his smile returns quickly. By second grade, he began to do brief slumps voluntarily.

It is possible that individuals may have learned to resist doing such behaviors, because they reveal one's inner state of being? Many may have been taught that such behaviors can be interpreted as signs of weakness, disrespect, or even aggression. However, we can begin to give these nonverbal behaviors much greater respect when we understand that they actually trigger a complex readjustment system that includes innervating the ventral vagus nerve networks. Even though these behaviors may indicate that an individual is experiencing a certain disruptive state, the movements may actually serve to decrease adrenalin. Then the individual returns fairly quickly to a state of rapport necessary for optimum engagement. As I mentioned before, one highly misunderstood behavior is the yawn.

Voice therapist Daniel Boone published the first book dedicated to voice disorders. The yawn/sigh approach (Boone, 1971:153-155) was explained as an effective strategy for individuals with hyperfunctional voice disorders. It enabled them to experience a more relaxed pitch and optimum voice quality as well as more appropriate loudness. The yawn is explained as a "prolonged inhalation with maximum widening of the supraglottal airway (characterized by a wide, stretching, opening of the mouth). The sigh is a gentle exhalation with "light phonation." Once the sigh was mastered, the easy phonation with a sigh is introduced. The sigh is followed by words beginning with [h] and combined with middle and low vowels.

Once voicing with gentle onset is mastered, the yawn is omitted and the breath is "a quicker, normal, open mouthed inhalation followed by the prolonged open-mouth sigh." Finally, once the yawn/sigh is mastered, the client would simply think of the relaxed feeling that the yawn/sigh produced. "Eventually, he will be able to maintain a relaxed phonation simply by imagining the approach" (Boone, 1971:154). This continues to be an effect approach for treating hyperfunctional voices. I now understand that it directly stimulates the ventral vagus nerve. How is it that this tactic works? Based on what you know so far, what is your answer?

Instead of creating a new hypothesis that required additional research, I realized that my answer had become reduced to a simple conclusion. It is what happens naturally when the ventral vagus nerve pathways are exercised through specific nonverbal language behaviors. This was no longer a hypothesis whereby I was looking at why or how a certain behavior reliably triggers a sense of wellbeing and enhanced rapport. Instead, it had become a consistent observation that others were benefiting from these voluntary nonverbal movements. If this was not a hypothesis, then it must be a theory. I decided to call the theory Nonverbal Language Integration. Yet, what is a theory?

I searched ASHA's publications and settled on "Commitment to Theory" (Friel-Patti, 1994), which addressed the recent introduction of auditory integration training (AIT), an "out-of-the-mainstream" clinical approach from France. Friel-Patti's focus was on what a theory is, why SLPs and audiologists should be committed to theory, and the importance of intervention research. AIT involved the modulation of musical sounds. Practitioners trained in the process insisted that the intervention worked for a wide variety of communication disorders. Why it worked was not considered to be important to the clinicians. However, "AIT doesn't make sense in light of any current model of auditory integration of information, music, or speech" (Friel-Patti, 1994:30).

"Theory provides a framework that is essential for understanding behaviors of interest and can serve as a rationale guide for intervention programming; however, given the inherent limitation of scope, theory may not encompass all aspects of behavior. . . . Commitment to theory is fundamental for building effective and efficient intervention programs" (Friel-Patti, 1994: 30, 31). In regard to research intervention, efficacy of a treatment is just as important as whether the process resulted in improvements. An efficacious approach means that the treatment is effective.

"Explicit discussion of reasons why something did or did not work helps to clarify the working hypothesis and governing theory. . . . The aim of treatment efficacy research is the measurement of change that can be attributed to the intervention" (Friel-Patti, 1994:31). According to Friel-Patti, ethnographic qualitative designs that use the participant/observer strategy are an acceptable form of scientific research. Some of these studies researched communication behavior in natural settings for hypothesis building rather than testing. "Such an inductive procedure permits the researcher to make open-ended observations and watch general patterns emerge; this approach contrasts sharply with the deductive approach of experimental design in which the dependent and independent variables are specified before data collection" (Friel-Patti, 1994:32, 33). ASHA now calls treatment efficacy research "evidence-based practice." I now felt assured that my use of an ethological (or ethnological) process is valid and efficacious research.

ASHA's Code of Ethics (2016) requires SLPs and audiologists to provide services that are based on ethical professional reasoning. Three rules of ethics especially apply to introducing a new theory.

1) Individuals shall accurately represent the intended purpose of a service, product, or research endeavor and shall abide by established guidelines for clinical practice and the responsible conduct of research.
2) Individuals who hold the Certificate of Clinical Competence shall evaluate the effectiveness of services provided, technology employed, and products dispensed, and they shall provide services or dispense products only when benefit can be reasonably expected.
3. Individuals who hold the Certificate of Clinical Competence shall use independent and evidence-based clinical judgment, keeping paramount the best interest of those being served.

Apel and Self (2003) provided guidelines for integrating research and clinical services into evidence-based practices. This means practitioners must "combine their clinical expertise with a body of specific research findings that are valid, reliable, and clinically relevant. By consciously seeking out and using scientific evidence as the foundation for their clinical services, SLPs and audiologists become clinical scientists." Clinical procedures are based on "specific rationale," and clinicians should "develop hypotheses for the clinical phenomena they encounter" rather than simply stating that it works (Apel and Self, 2003:6). What this actually means is that clinicians are constantly in a mode of learning. This means therapy services involve an ongoing process of assessing outcomes in order to develop new hypotheses regarding procedures and responses, including rapport and neuroplasticity. Learning is a lifelong commitment in order to be aware of scientific research that offers new insights into "clinical phenomena."

I now felt confident that Nonverbal Language Integration is a theory that evolved from an evidence-based practice approach. This guidebook demonstrates both an inductive qualitative design of observation and a deductive approach, which was based on literature review. Unlike AIT, Nonverbal Language Integration is *not* an "out-of-the-mainstream approach." It addresses important communication behaviors that individuals across the lifespan already engage in. This involves our nonverbal language.

Improving nonverbal language (pragmatics) is already an efficacious approach in speech-language therapy. Nonverbal Language Integration offers a new theory regarding the role nonverbal language behaviors play in generating homeostasis and establishing rapport. It provides new information that clients and families can be taught using simple terms. This information includes the neurophysiology behind these innate nonverbal behaviors and how to "use" them as tools to optimize interpersonal communication and enhance rapport. Rapport is important for successful learning outcomes. Understanding the theory requires more than having knowledge regarding the neurophysiology involved in assessing and activating the vagus nerve. Chapter Twelve explains what the theory of Nonverbal Language Integration is about.

Twelve

THE THEORY OF NONVERBAL LANGUAGE INTEGRATION

As clinicians, in addition to changing linguistic behavior, we are changing a vehicle by which one initiates, maintains, and terminates relationships with others.
Carol Prutting (1982:129)

Nonverbal language involves behaviors that convey meaning, but the thoughts and feelings are not being expressed through the actual words. It includes facial expressions, hand and arm gestures, postures, positions and various movements of the body or the legs or the feet (Harper, et al., 1978:20). Nonverbal behaviors also include paralinguistics, whereby meaning is conveyed through the voice by the modification of vocal qualities (vocalizations). These nonverbal expressions occur in many vertebral species, while verbal communication is a specialized system unique to humans. Yet, vocalizations can be nonverbal when "nonverbal" means that words are not being used to represent something semantically.

The field of speech-language pathology calls this area pragmatics. "As clinicians, in addition to changing linguistic behavior, we are changing a vehicle by which one initiates, maintains, and terminates relationships with others (Prutting, 1982:129). Prutting discusses pragmatics as actually indicating social competence. In this way, pragmatics is this vehicle and its purpose is social interaction. Pragmatics involves a highly developed structure involving "nonverbal communication codes of attitudes and emotions in social interaction which support, complement, or replace verbal behavior. These nonverbal components include such behaviors as bodily contact, posture, gaze, physical appearances, facial and gestural movements, as well as paralinguistic aspects such as tone, timing, and accent" (Prutting, 1982:131).

I taught English pronunciation to employees at a Fortune 500 company during the 1990's and created the workbook and accompanying audiotapes. I believe the high success was because I stressed that the pragmatics of voice is an important factor for clear communication. The Mehrabian equation of communication, especially in cases of dislike, theorizes that the intensity of a message is 7% verbal feeling, 38% vocal feeling, and 55% facial feeling (Mehrabian, 1972:182). "Vocal feeling" includes the paralinguistics of intonation, emphasis, stress, and pauses. Intonation involves pitch frequencies and two styles of pitch changes: inflections and shifts. Inflections are fluid and singsong-like changes in pitch. They indicate that a topic is open for informal discussion and negotiation. Shifts have slight breaks between the pitch changes both within syllables and between words. A shift signals a more assertive intention; the topic is not open for discussion. Stressing words within sentences by pitch change and increased duration creates emphasis, which decreases the risk of ambiguities. Pauses (or silence between words) set the tempo and help to convey the importance or complexity of the message to the listener.

Within nonverbal language, vocalizations can be "arranged along a continua such as laughing, giggling, snickering, whimpering, sobbing, and crying. Other vocal characteristics would include yelling, muttering, muffled sounds, and whispering; moaning and groaning; yawning and belching; whining and voice breaking" (Harper, et.al., 1978: 21). These are not solely "vocalizations," because they are accompanied by a continuum of facial expressions and gestures as well. From my experience with neurologically impaired adults, I would add obscenities. This is because the utterances, and accompanying facial expressions and gestures, are automatic behaviors that bypass the specialized cerebral processing required for verbal language. Swearing can remain intact in those with acquired severe speech and/or language deficits. The words are not being used to represent concrete or abstract concepts but rather serve to express frustration. I observed that obscenities produce that same omohyoid muscle tension.

Even more importantly, because the ventral vagus nerve is involved in the motor production as well as sensory reception of these actions, it makes great sense that venting behaviors help to calm the speaker. This gives a new perspective to the value of venting through the use of "pet" swear words as well as certain facial expressions, gestures, and postures that are perceived to be socially negative. It may not be the negative meaning behind the profanity or body language that is important. Instead, it is very likely that these nonverbal actions, vocal and gestures, are activating the ventral vagus nerve to re-establish a calmer state and greater presence of mind. From this perspective, a multitude of "negative" nonverbal language behaviors within the realm of pragmatics serve as a "vagus brake" to reset the autonomic nervous system. Since nonverbal language pragmatics exist in humans regardless of culture, they can be viewed as phylogenetically evolved behaviors that activate the parasympathetic nervous system (ventral vagus nerve pathways). These pathways automatically defuse stressful feelings in order to reset the intention of awareness, attention, and focus to be for engaging in authentic rapport.

With this in mind, I realized that I had developed a theory that I could not find mentioned in research literature. The Q Collar sparked hypotheses, and the development of the theory resulted from combining my knowledge and clinical experiences as a SLP since 1976. This also includes over two decades in management as Director of Speech Pathology and Audiology at Alameda County Medical Center in California, which requires competency in compliance. I also drew upon my training and experience required for my D.Min. and ordination as an Interfaith minister.

Nonverbal Language Integration is the name best suited because it integrates sensory systems with the motor behaviors of pragmatics to exercise the ventral vagus nerve pathways. I mentioned that I began to visualize this project within the metaphor of an ancient underground river with underground streams and above-the-ground springs. The river is the ventral vagus nerve according to the Polyvagal Theory by Stephen Porges, Ph.D. The streams had become the variety of internal systems that the vagus nerve is involved with. I realized that I had been searching for a visible spring that I could access based on my knowledge and skills. That spring percolated pragmatics, or nonverbal language behaviors.

Gestures, facial expressions, and vocalizations that fit within nonverbal language behaviors do more than clarify the speaker's intent of the message. They also convey the sender's state of emotion. "Nonverbal cues are the principal means of expressing basic affective or emotive states" (Mortensen, 1972:217). These expressions can occur unconsciously and consciously on a continuum of no awareness to high attention. These behaviors communicate "the most personal of all types of communication. . . with which the body makes its self disclosures." Effective communication requires that the listener and speaker be able to make inferences about each other's feelings, intentions, desires, knowledge, and even beliefs.

For decades, neuroscience has been showing that nonverbal language behaviors have a contagious element due to some innate neural phenomena many call mirror neurons. Neurologist and neuroscientist Marco Iacoboni defines the longstanding "facial feedback hypothesis" to be the theory that "emotional experience is shaped by changes in facial musculature" (Iacoboni, 2008:120). According to Iacoboni, inner mirroring occurs effortlessly, automatically, and unconsciously when we observe the expressions of others.

According to researchers Wicker et al. "observing the facial expression of another evokes a similar facial motor expression in the observer" (2003:655). Wicker et al.'s core finding was that the left anterior insula was activated when observing disgust or smelling a disgusting odor. They reported that other research has shown that electrical stimulation of the left anterior insula has triggered negative sensations in the throat and mouth.

With this information in mind, it is very likely that negative sensations in the throat trigger negative facial expressions, which then trigger the ventral vagus nerve in both the sender and receiver of a message. This would help insure that both participants are engaging the vagal breaking process in a way that promotes venting and reciprocity for enhanced rapport. If so, this would inhibit the sympathetic nervous system from escalating the situation into a fight or causing one to flee.

The vagal break also inhibits the dorsal vagus nerve from creating the state of immobilization. From this perspective, certain nonverbal language behaviors viewed as venting would be phylogenic behaviors that evolved to de-escalate conflict through automatic reactions that actually activate the ventral vagus nerve. That would mean the purpose for these "negative" nonverbal behaviors is not to increase stress among individuals or within one's self. Instead, they would be activating the vagus nerve pathways that return the individuals to homeostasis and promote the states of equilibrium and socially engaged rapport necessary for survival and success.

From this perspective of venting, my grandson's reaction of slumped shoulders and bowed head creates the same sensation of immobilization in others. This would be an important innate survival tactic when immobilization was crucial. Yet, when no real threat exists, such mirroring can cause a "contagious" frustration in others. Understanding these behaviors as venting that ultimately re-establishes homeostasis can "lighten up" the situation for everyone. This is what I observe happen each time I reminded my grandson that he just activated his vagus nerve.

Activation of the ventral vagus nerve returns the body's system to the positive state required for rest, digestion, oxygenation, and social interactions. This helps insure the return to positive intrapersonal communication, which is so important to the health, growth, and success of social units from personal relationships within families to large institutions. While we may not be able to choose how our body reacts to a certain situation initially, we do have choice in learning how to exercise the ventral vagus nerve to prepare for the next situation. This can be accomplished by using many nonverbal actions that are "discouraged" because of their innate potential to signal a warning and, therefore, create a sense of discomfort. Nonverbal language behaviors that fall under grieving, aggression, or "giving up" would be more highly respected if their role in returning each individual, from infants to the elderly, to positive states necessary for rapport was better understood.

Learning often results after something negative happened. Just as the yawn and swallow can be reflexive or voluntary, we can learn to recognize "venting" behaviors and use them to alert ourselves that something stressful but not actually life threatening has happened. Then we can actually use these nonverbal behaviors voluntarily as tools that recruit ventral vagus nerve pathways that optimize rapport. Being in an optimal state of rapport enhances learning abilities from attention and concentration to memory and skill development. This is a paradigm shift that I am identifying as the theory of Nonverbal Language Integration. It is not just a philosophical supposition. The theory includes many natural nonverbal language behaviors that can be used as exercises to tone the vagus nerve. Guidelines for the exercises follow in Chapter Thirteen.

Thirteen

GENERAL GUIDELINES
FOR USING NONVERBAL LANGUAGE EXERCISES

Yet, rapport has moved beyond social graces with the clinician acting friendly and competent. It happens naturally and authentically between the clinician and client because both have exercised the ventral vagus nerve.

This guidebook acknowledges that SLPs, audiologists, and other rehabilitation related clinicians and specialists are well trained in how to lead clients in doing exercises that improve motor, behavioral, emotional, cognitive, and even spiritual functioning. Therefore, the process of instruction, drill, and measuring progress are not addressed in this guidebook. Each clinician is trained in the therapeutic process based on a scope of practice. The specific skills addressed depend on the clinician's area of expertise. As in most clinical situations, reporting is subjective and objective. The observation of the results is based on the knowledge and experience of the clinician as well as the client's perception regarding outcomes. From this perspective, client self-reporting becomes an important indicator of progress towards specific goals as well as the clinician's observation of any shifts in the client's learning state and the level of rapport established.

In clinical documentation, the exercises, nerves, or muscles are generally not addressed when writing goals or documenting progress. This also holds true when exercise are done to establish rapport at the beginning of a session. Goals and progress are identified in functional terms regarding the skills necessary to function at optimal levels in everyday activities of life. You may recognize some of the exercises as warm-up activities prior to engaging in more mentally challenging tasks. Some of the results from using these exercises for enhancing rapport with communicatively impaired adults during one workweek are shared in Chapter Thirteen: Case Examples.

Assessment begins by educating clients and/or families on the reasons for the evaluation, including its risks and benefits. Therapy begins with explanations of the techniques, evidence of their validity in helping to resolve a problem or develop a new skill, and the rationale for engaging in further practice. It was my intention to provide more than enough data regarding the vagus nerve system in order that the theory, its rationale, and exercises to enhance rapport can be applied to a wide variety of practices. Each clinician can extract data from this guidebook that is most applicable for their clients. For this reason, I have provided only one example script at the end of this chapter for instructing clients on the theory of Nonverbal Language Integration.

In regard to the exercises, the Nonverbal Language Integration behaviors for activating the ventral vagus nerve pathways are organized into three areas: cognitive, motor, and sensory. The first area, cognitive, begins with the importance of using cues to reinforce learning. Then two exercises focus on engaging the imagination (imagery). It is well known in sports medicine that imagining doing an action activates and helps to tone the nerves responsible for the skill as well aiding in endurance and recovery. Research on the yawn (Chapter Seven) shows that it activates the precuneus, which is responsible for motor imagery at the very least. Metaphors, such as idioms and analogies, can enhance the imagination by sparking creativity within the right side of the brain. Reflecting on common metaphors that represent how specific nonverbal behaviors are associated with feelings can help to reinforce that these motor and sensory exercises activate the ventral vagus nerve.

Categories for motor behaviors include: 1) body postures and gestures 2) facial expressions 3) oral actions 4) non-speech vocalizations 5) prosody and 6) articulation of certain vowels and consonants. Categories for sensory stimulation include: 1) tactile and 2) auditory. Exercises for sensory awareness help bring individuals into the present moment and prepare them for sensing how the different nonverbal behaviors make them feel. While these exercises are not all inclusive, this is the first guidebook to my knowledge that offers specific nonverbal exercises with the goal of activating ventral vagus nerve pathways to enhance rapport. I am certain that you will think of other nonverbal language behaviors after going through the exercises.

It is important to tell the client that the intention of the exercises is to activate the ventral vagus nerve in order to be in the state of equilibrium, which is necessary to achieve the functional goals for that session. Yet, my observations and research of the literature suggest that a toned system of vagus nerve pathways will enhance the states of learning required for positive social engagement, skill mastery, and wellness.

It is important to remember that wellness does not necessarily mean that a diagnosis is reversed. Wellness means that the individual is engaging life with an autonomic nervous system that is balanced in regard to sympathetic and parasympathetic activation. Another term for such wellness is resilience. One immediate effect that I have noticed is that frustration, self-blame, and blaming others in regard to making errors are reduced. The exercises have no right or wrong way to do them. Just doing the nonverbal behaviors consciously in one's own way has been demonstrated to make a difference that is beneficial.

General Script for Introducing Nonverbal Language Integration

The following script can be adapted to meet your client's needs by adding, deleting, or rearranging content. Before presenting this information to a client, I suggest that you practice it with a family member or friend. As the content becomes more familiar, you may even want think about how to act out some examples. I have used emergency drills called over the hospital's PA system. I act out initially "freezing" to the alert, then deciding which direction to go (flight/fight), and finally returning to a sense of calm when it is announced that the drill is over.

Have you heard of our systems going into fight or flight? This has to do with the autonomic nervous system, which is functioning all the time without our awareness. When something disruptive happens, our body produces adrenalin. That causes us to move into a higher state of stress in preparation for powerful action. If a true danger exists, we will either fight or run away. This is the sympathetic nervous system. If there is no immediate threat to our safety, our nervous system is designed to move back into a state of ease. This is the parasympathetic nervous system. At one time it was believed we would only be in one of these two states. But that has changed.

Have you heard of the Polyvagal Theory by Stephen Porges? It says that three stages are involved. The sympathetic nervous system of flight or fight reactions (like a rapid heartbeat) is triggered by fear and adrenalin. But first, the parasympathetic state of immobilization is triggered by the dorsal vagus nerve. This action of freezing or being motionless happens when something different happens or there is a threat. It is the most primitive reaction and occurs first.

The second system within the parasympathetic nervous system is regulated by the ventral vagus nerve. The ventral vagus nerve returns the body and mind to a state of balance for optimal rapport and social engagement by putting a brake on the adrenalin (and slows the heartbeat). Instead of being in one state or the other, there needs to be a healthy balance between the sympathetic and parasympathetic nervous systems. This is called equilibrium, which is the natural state for social engagement, concentration, focus, healthy imagination, interpersonal communication, and learning.

However, when something happens to us, our system can get out of balance. The body and mind may begin to spend too much time in the fight or flight states or in the immobilized state due to the dorsal vagus nerve. The ventral vagus nerve loses it tone just like muscles do when they are not used. What most people do not realize is that there are certain natural behaviors that actually activate the ventral vagus nerve.

I am sorry about what happened to you, but I want you to know that the worst is over. You are now ready to do what needs to be done to get better. However, in order to get through your ordeal, your body has had to go into longer periods of fight or flight and even immobilization in order for you to manage up to this point. Now, if you are ready, it is time to begin to activate your vagus nerve pathways in order for the healthy balance to be reset. One way to begin is with the yawn.

Surprisingly, neuroscience has discovered that yawn has been quite misunderstood. Instead of it being a sign of boredom, the yawn is actually a natural behavior that activates the vagus nerve. It also stimulates the precuneus, the area of the brain that promotes attention, focus, memory, motor planning, and reasoning. I would like you to yawn just like I am doing now. Now, yawn with me face-to-face and then tell me how you feel afterwards. There are other behaviors that activate it as well. Lets do a progressive vagus nerve activation exercise together so you can experience them. It goes from your toes to the top of your head. Think of how you feel now, and then I will ask you again after the exercise.

I have found that few individuals can yawn face-to-face, and the activity often makes the client smile. I have observed individuals to have a more positive outlook and participate with a more focused mindset to succeed after doing the progressive vagus nerve activation exercise on pages 92-93. This suggests that rapport has been established, which then enhances motivation to participate. In this way, rapport has moved beyond social graces with the clinician acting friendly, caring, and competent. It happens naturally and authentically between the clinician and client, because both have exercised the ventral vagus nerve. The same is true when family members or caregivers are instructed as well.

In regard to the exercises that are included in Chapter Fourteen, many are behaviors and even cognitive tasks that are instructed by speech-language pathologists. The postures and gestures may be exercised during physical therapy, occupational therapy, and even patient activities. What is important to remember is that the intention for doing the activities is to exercise the vagus nerve for improving rapport. Maintaining authentic rapport is an important component of every session with a client. However, rapport is not documented. Instead, the client's level of motivation, the client's perception of the formal treatment, and the functional outcomes from the session are documented. The information provided within a script and the exercises can be used as content when instructing in memory strategies and following directions within sessions.

Fourteen

NONVERBAL LANGUAGE EXERCISES FOR INNERVATING THE VENTRAL VAGUS NERVE

Instead, the muscles that trigger the vagus break are specifically targeted.

MOTOR EXERCISES

Certain postures, gestures, and facial expressions occur spontaneously to a situation when we are uncertain about how to proceed. These can be interpreted along a continuum from not caring about the topic to being angry, frightened, or sad about it. Besides alerting us to our feelings, these behaviors can be acknowledged as important indicators that a challenge has caused adrenalin to rise. When no immediate danger is present, the body is naturally working to reestablish homeostasis because greater attention is warranted. The actions stimulate the ventral vagus nerve pathways just enough to activate the vagus brake. This results in lowering the self-protective reactions of the sympathetic nervous system of flight or fight or the dorsal vagus nerve's immobilization impulse.

Body posturing and facial expressions are not exercised as repetitive actions. Instead, the positions are held for ten seconds. Have the client hold the position until a sigh is produced, or hopefully, even a yawn. Encourage the client to pay attention to the muscles being used as well as the inner sensation that arise, especially when the tension is released. This fits with the well-accepted practice of progressive relaxation (page 92); tensing one muscle at a time and then relaxing it to relieve overall tension. Instead, the muscles that trigger the vagus break are specifically targeted.

Postures and Gestures

Entwine the fingers on both hands and extend the palms outward.

Cross the index and middle fingers on each hand.

Clench the fists at specific levels to the body (hips, chest, shoulders, above head)

Press the palms together.

Shrug the shoulders.

Cross the entwined arms across the chest like a self-hug.

Cross arms and press on arms just below the shoulders.

Extend the toes upward similar to the standing on tiptoe position. (Avoid clenching the toes).

Walk by pushing off with the toes.

Swing crossed feet back and forth under a chair.

Whole body shaking to just shaking the hands.

Posture is upright so that the ears are in the middle of the shoulder.

    Stand at "attention" with arms at sides.

    Stand "at ease" with arms behind the back.

Stand on tiptoe and peek to one side.

Place hand on top of the head and/or tap the head.

Facial Expressions

Gaze without direct focus.

Stare forward at an object with eyebrows slightly raised.

Keeping the head forward, look far up to the right or left (as if peeking).

Close the eyes tightly.

Squint.

Grimace.

Scream silently.

Widen the nose.

Sniff (which widens the nostrils).

Stick out the tongue with the tip pointed from midline and towards the chin.

Purse the lips.

Stick the chin out.

Oral Movements

Most oral behaviors are difficult to hold because of being repetitive movements. Encourage the client to do the movements slowly and pay attention to the muscles being engaged and the inner sensations that arise.

Blow.

Chew.

Clench the jaw.

Gargle.

Gulp.

Kiss.

Spit.

Suck.

Swallow.

Smack lips.

Pucker, smack, and blow a kiss.

Non-Speech Vocalizations

Cough.

Cry.

Hack.

Hum.

Gasp

Sneeze.

Throat clear.

Wail.

Valsalva Maneuver: Attempting to exhale against a closed airway

Progressive Vagus Nerve Activation Exercise

Progressive relaxation involves the tightening and release of muscles. It is an evidence-based exercise to reduce tension. Edward Jacobson introduced "progressive relaxation" exercises in the 1938, "whereby an individual induces relaxation at some point in his body and allows it to spread progressively until total relaxation has been achieved" (DiCarlo, 1974:390). I first began using progressive relaxation techniques in the mid 1970's with patients who had laryngectomees. Since then, I have integrated shortened versions into my treatment sessions with many of my clients. This is what inspired me to develop this progressive exercise of ventral vagus nerve activation. However, instead of focusing on tightening and relaxing muscle groups, it progressively combines behaviors selected from the previous exercises. The following script combines the exercises from the toes to the top of the head with the goal of activating the system in a balanced manner that promotes a sense of heightened rapport. The rational is included with each behavior. This can be included or deleted based on each client. Also, the client being able to state the rationale shows learning.

Before leading the client in the exercise for the first time, you may want the individual to "measure" his/her current sensations of stress using a 0-10 scale. The 0 represents no stress and a complete sense of calmness and readiness. The number 10 represents the most extreme sense of stress that is also highly disruptive. Then ask the client to rate the level of stress and sense of readiness after doing the exercise.

Focus on your toes and bring them towards your nose. Imagine you are standing on tiptoe. We must be calm to stretch and reach up for something. Hold the toes-to-the-nose position for a count of ten.

Now, bring your focus upwards to your lower belly. Imagine that you are preventing yourself from urinating. This is called a Kegel. We have to be calm when looking for a bathroom. Hold for a count of ten.

Bring your focus to your diaphragm. Take a deep breath and then sigh out through pursed lips. Keep the diaphragm still for a count of five. We hold our breath to prepare to fight or run. We let it out and do not breathe in momentarily after everything is all clear

Now, bring your attention to your heart. Imagine that you can feel the beat of your heart. Research shows that people who are aware of heartbeats have less stress. Imagine counting ten heartbeats.

Produce one slow long yawn followed by a sigh. The yawn activates the precuneus.

Focus on your nose and widen your nostrils while imagining smelling an interesting aroma. Breathe in slowly.

Keep your head facing forward. Move your eyes to the far right and hold for a count of ten. Now, move your eyes to the left and hold for a count of ten. We must remain calm when multitasking, such as looking forward while also glancing to the side to see what is happening.

Move your attention to just above your nose and between your eyebrows. Hold an inquisitive frown for a count of ten. We must be calm to concentrate on something new that interests us.

And now, pretend to sneeze. Notice how you bring your toes towards you nose, do a Kegel, tighten your diaphragm, wrinkle you nose, and furrow your brow for a long "ah" followed by release during the short "chew."

Allowing your focus to go to the top of your head, gently pat yourself on the head for having exercised your vagus nerve pathways. This relates to the dive reflex, which protects the brain by preventing slosh.

COGNITIVE

Cues

An important indicator of a client's progress is the kind of assistance required to accomplish a newly learned skill. Assistance is provided through cues that are generally measured based on a hierarchical continuum of tactile, visual, and auditory triggers. Visual cues, which have been demonstrated to assist in motor skill development, usually begin with those actions that the individual can imitate. Once the client understands the basic concepts of Nonverbal Language Integration and the gestures that activate ventral vagus nerve pathways, have the client observe those behaviors in others.

Television offers a rich source of nonverbal language behaviors. These "cues" can be imitated and even discussed in terms of what circumstances may have triggered the behavior and how the behavior served to activate the ventral vagus nerve pathways. Doing this exercise while watching professional basketball with Chuck, a dedicated Golden State Warriors fan, has given me an even greater appreciation of how nonverbal language behaviors are used to return individuals to a state of homeostasis. This includes the player, the fan watching the game from home, and the spouse watching the fan. Most hospitalized patients have screens on their walls. This gives patients and their families an activity to do together that actually has the potential to trigger the ventral vagus nerve pathways that promote their rapport with each other.

Imagery

Imagery can trigger the sensory systems that stimulate the ventral vagus nerve pathways that bring us into the present moment. Thinking about chocolate chips cookies baking can make the nostrils widen. Have the client trigger the various senses voluntarily. Look around the setting and notice four things that can be seen. Listen to the sounds and notice four things that are heard. Feel for four things that can be touched. Imagine smelling four aromas. Image tasting four flavors. Imagine feeling ten heartbeats.

Metaphors

Metaphors can give us insights into natural biological movements that produce consistent sensations. "Metaphors draw upon the elementary and familiar aspects of sensory-perceptual experiences, whose rich connotations provide the basis for understanding the novel (as in science) and the unfamiliar (as in learning)" (Mehrabian, 1972:181). There are idioms for gestures, facial expression, and speech that can represent either calming oneself, remaining calm, and the inability to calm oneself when facing a challenge, or taking responsibility. Metaphors are used in cognitive language therapy to improve inductive reasoning (making broader generalizations from a specific detail). Instead of working with metaphors that have little to do with the body, such as "Every cloud has a silver lining," using metaphors that relate to actions can trigger the ventral vagus nerve as well.

Blow a kiss.
Breathe a sigh of relief.
Kiss goodbye.
Kiss off.
Kiss up to someone.
Kisses sweeter than wine.
Sealed with a kiss.
By the skin of your teeth.
Chewing something over.
Clear your throat.
Clenched fist of truth.
Cool one's heels.
Cry your heart out.
Hem and haw.
Hum with activity.
I'm all ears.
Have the neck to do something.
Neck with.
Pain in the neck.
Nose is out of joint.
Follow one's nose.
Look down one's nose.
Stick one's nose in.
Turn one's nose up.

Put one foot in front of the other.
Pull one's leg.
To foot the bill.
See eye to eye.
Shrug it off.
Shake it off.
Shake in one's shoes.
Not to be sneezed at.
Sniff it out.
Stick your neck out.
Suck it up.
Swallow your pride.
Hard to swallow.
Stick your chin out.
Stick your neck out.
Toe the line.
Throat.

ARTICULATION

By now the client is aware of the area of the omohyoid muscle and tension in the neck during postural and facial expression movements. These articulation exercises are not for the purpose of improving speech. While they can be incorporated into articulation therapy and voice therapy by an SLP, the purpose within this guidebook is the activation of the vagus nerve for rapport. These vowels and consonants produce tension in the area of the omohyoid muscle with the least effort. The purpose of the articulation exercise is for the client to become aware of this tension and any feelings that follow the production of each sound or word.

Have the client touch the neck while firmly saying the following sounds, vowels, consonants, and words. How does the client feel after saying the sounds and words? What happens in the neck when the client imagines saying the sounds or words? How does the client feel after saying each sound and after saying each word.

Animal sounds: "Grrr," like a bear. "Ruff," like a dog. "Rrarr," like a lion. "Heehaw," like a donkey. Crow like a rooster.

Vowels: ah, ae (like "had"), ai (as in "I"], ee, eh (like head), er, ih (as in "if"), o (like oh), uh. Prolong the vowels for five seconds.

Consonants: d, dj (as in judge) f, g, h, l, m, n, ng, r, sh, y, z. Say each consonant firmly.

Consonant plus vowel:

Dough Duh Dye Jaw Gee Guy Foe Go Her Low My Gnaw Knee No Raw Rye Show Shy Yeah

Vowel plus consonant:

Odd Add I'd Al Am Anne Ash As If Eel Ed Egg Earl Urge Ode Oaf Ohm Own Ugh Um

Consonant plus vowel plus consonant:

Dang Dodge Dog Doll Dawn Dad Dyed Did Dig Dead Deal Dim Din Dish Deed Dome Dud Dug Dull Done Dung Does

Jog John Jot Jam Jazz Germ Gem Jill Jim Jones Judge

Fog Fall Fawn Fad Fang Fan Fowl Fife Fine Feed Feel Fein Firm Fish Fizz Foam Fudge Fun Fern Fuzz

Gang God Gag Gal Gash Guide Guys Girl Gill Gong

Hog Had Hag Ham Harsh Hide Hire Heed Heel Head Hem Hen Here Hurl Herd Hole Home Hone Hose Hug Huff Hull Hum Hung Hush

Log Long Lad Lamb Lash Lied Lime Liar Lead League Lean Leash Ledge Learn Lid Limb Liz Load Lug Lung Lush

Mod Mall Mad Man Mar Mash Marsh Mars Mime Mine Mire Mead Meal Mean Mel Men Mid Mill Mirror

Nag Gnash Knife Nile Kneel Ned Nell Nerd Node Gnome Nose Nudge Numb None

Rod Ron Roz Rad Rag Ram Ran Rang Rash Razz Raid Rage Rail Rain Rare Raise Reed Reef Reel Ream Red Rid Rig Rim Road Rogue Roam Roan Rose Ruff Rum Run Rung Rush

Shall Sham Shawl Shine She'd Sheen She's Sure Shim Showed Shoal Shone Shows

Yawn Yam Yams Yale Yang Yank Yarn Yarns Yauld Yawl Yean Year Years Yearn Yearns Yegg Yell Yields Yins You'd Young Your Yodel Yogi Yogurt

SENSORY EXERCISES

Sensory stimulation can be done with individuals who are not able to follow directions. Clients can also be instructed to do sensory stimulation with their own bodies.

Tactile

Instruct the client to do the following actions. If there is paralysis, have the client imagine doing them.

Tap the balls of the feet.

Gently press the toes towards the nose.

Press down on the shoulders with opposite hands.

Place the fingertips on the sides of the neck just above the collarbone.

Place the fingertips on face and thumbs under chin.

Pinch the nose.

Place the palm of the hand on the forehead.

Tap the head just above the forehead.

Cup hands behind the ears.

Tap the top of the head (also known as the diving reflex).

Place the hand on the belly, and do a Kegel ("hold" the urine).

Place a hand on the chest. Imagine being aware of ten heartbeats.

Fifteen

CASE EXAMPLES

The eight patients who did listen about the vagus nerve and participated in the specific nonverbal language exercises left me feeling invigorated. I hypothesized that this was not as much about gains but because I was stimulating my own vagus nerve along with them.

"The ASHA Leader" had a timely article (Robertson, 2019) that not only gave me permission but also motivated me to continue exploring integrating nonverbal language into speech-language therapy for the purpose of activating vagus nerve pathways to enhance rapport. Sheri Robertson, Ph.D. had recently retired from her position as a professor in the Department of Communication Disorders at Indiana University of Pennsylvania. She stressed that there are speech-language pathologists and audiologists who are "imaginologists." "They routinely flex their creativity muscles to drive our profession forward by imagining more and imagining better for the patients, clients, and students" (2019:6). Robertson stressed that imagination generates innovation and quoted Einstein: "Imagination is the preview of life's coming attractions." She advised that we "can build our capacity to imagine more and imagine better" by moving away from "if only" and towards "what if there was a way to inspire…" (2019:7). This perspective provided me with a better understanding regarding what I had been behaving like since reading about the compression collar in July 2018. I have been an imaginologist.

In May 2019, I worked a week at the hospital where I have been employed since 2002 as the per diem SLP. This gave me the opportunity to share the theory of nonverbal language integration and some exercises with patients hospitalized for respiratory failure. I observed the impact on rapport over a five-day period. Due to confidentiality laws, I have provided minimal medical information about these cases, which includes quadriplegia from a motor vehicle accident, cognitive language disorders and dysphagia from cerebral vascular accidents, to oral cancer. What was most important to me is that, regardless of the diagnosis, eight out of ten patients showed gains beyond what they achieved from standard practices when the vagus nerve pathways were not activated a means of enhancing rapport.

Coincidently, on Monday, I had to complete "compliance training" on standards of truth when reporting the outcomes of treatment. The national organizations of rehabilitation disciplines all set standards for addressing quality of care and accuracy of reporting. According to ASHA's rules of ethics "Individuals shall not engage in dishonesty, fraud, deceit, or misrepresentation." According to the Center for Medicare Services, the decision regarding whether to continue to provide care is based on outcomes of prior treatments. Outcomes are used to help capture the patient's status, set goals, and to determine if an intervention is effective. Accuracy in assessing performance and documenting results is crucial for insuring correct care of patients. The supervisor was surprised that I became excited over the content and asked for a copy. I realized that this is what I was striving for during this entire process of researching the vagus nerve pathways in relationship to nonverbal behaviors, rapport, and reporting observations. I have abided by these same standards in sharing the effects of teaching the vagus nerve system and nonverbal behaviors to ten patients.

The two patients that did not show improvements in participation were being treated for pharyngeal/laryngeal phase dysphagia. One was a man in his sixties with a right brain CVA that required a craniotomy. He had a history of alcoholism and impulsivity prior to onset. The other was a woman in her forties with chronic COPD and schizophrenia who easily became verbally abusive. Both patients denied having swallowing difficulties and were not interested in learning strategies for safe swallows. Both continued to eat impulsively and ignore verbal cues. Both refused to participate in structured exercises.

However, what I did discover from these two patients is that the nonverbal strategies for enhancing rapport helped me. In the past, I may have become frustrated by their noncompliance and denial and would have "acted" the part of being empathic, understanding, and benevolent. Instead, by engaging in my own nonverbal behaviors that activate the return to homeostasis, I discovered that I remained authentically engaged and optimistic. While the two patients continued to deny swallow problems, they engaged me with more appropriate social behavior than was their norm. We had been in rapport. I left their rooms feeling refreshed rather than drained.

The eight patients who did listen about the vagus nerve and participated in the specific nonverbal language exercises left me feeling invigorated. I hypothesized that this was not as much about gains but because I was stimulating my own vagus nerve along with them. These eight case examples are as follows:

1) An elderly woman, following a motor vehicle accident two weeks prior, suffered quadriplegia, facial bruising, and respiratory failure requiring a tracheostomy. She was weaning from mechanical ventilation when I saw her. The

patient was communicating with yes/no head gestures to questions and weakly mouthing words. In the past, I might have postponed treatment until she was stronger, or at least ready for the Passy Muir Valve when no longer requiring the ventilator. Instead, I did tactile stimulation of her neck and face and physically moved her fingers and feet in nonverbal language positions that are consistent with innervating the omohyoid muscle. I instructed the family in doing these exercises after explaining the Nonverbal Language Integration theory. They became excited and expressed that the theory made great sense. By the fifth day, the patient was wiggling her toes and fingertips and range of motion of her lips and tongue had increased. While this may have been a coincidence, no harm was done. Each family member expressed feeling hopeful and grateful to have something to do that might benefit the patient. This indicates that they were in states of authentic rapport with their loved one.

2) A middle-aged man with tongue cancer had an anterior glossectomy with reconstruction surgery. He had a tracheostomy due to airway obstruction. He continued to require a PEG for nutrition due to a distaste for most foods as well as oral dysphagia. His speech required careful listening, and he often made excuses as to why he could not eat or speak. He had been employed as a college professor. Rather than just teaching traditional strategies and counseling, I explained the Polyvagal Theory and how using nonverbal behaviors that stimulate the vagus nerve may, very likely, enhance rapport both with others and intrapersonally.

Instead of using everyday topics to exercise speech sounds in conversation, we engaged in discussions about the vagus nerve pathways and the role in returning the body to states of homeostasis required for optimum learning and skill mastery. We explored these possibilities during oral motor exercises that I have also identified to tense the omohyoid muscle. By the end of five days, his production of the lingua velar k and g phonemes had improved in structured speech, spontaneous speech intelligibility had improved, intraoral pressure for audible lip smacking had increased, and he began tasting more of the foods brought on his tray. He began telling me about articles he found on the Internet about the vagus nerve. His improvements were more significant that I had anticipated. He no longer made excuses as to why he could not try something. Successful rapport had been established.

3) A young woman in her thirties had a basal ganglion CVA as well as a past right hemisphere CVA. Memory and attention were impaired. Initially her respiratory failure required a tracheostomy and mechanical ventilation. She was now with a t-piece and on room oxygen. She had oral dysphagia and pharyngeal dysphagia with poor clearing of residue following the swallow. She was having

two pureed snacks a day with supervision. Her voice volume was poor for clear speech and mouth opening was often limited even though she could open her mouth wider when provided with visual and tactile cues. She was unable to recall any of the swallow strategies or exercises that were reviewed each session.

The patient's sister, who is in healthcare, was very assertive and mildly confrontational. I told the client and sister about the Polyvagal Theory and the theory about nonverbal behaviors being used to stimulate the vagus nerve. I instructed the patient in a variety of techniques to create an enhanced state of rapport, which is important for learning. The sister was very positive about the information and said that it made great sense.

After instructing the patient in a few nonverbal behaviors for enhancing rapport, I paired them with vocal fold abduction exercises as well as coordinating the behaviors with breath support. Voice volume increased almost immediately in response. Mouth opening widened for vowels, which were prolonged longer. The next day, the patient recalled three nonverbal language behaviors that she was using to speak louder and swallow more firmly. She said she felt more positive over all. The patient was decannulated on Thursday, and I did a Modified Barium Swallow study on Friday with all levels of food consistencies. The swallow was delayed but there was only minimally trace residue in the oral and pharyngeal cavity after the swallows. She was upgraded to Level 5 (moist/minced) snacks. Her overall voice volume increased and mouth opening widened with verbal cues. She had become more socially engaged.

4) A middle-age woman suffered sudden onset acute respiratory failure that had initially required a tracheostomy and mechanical ventilation. She was now decannulated. She was a manager of a department and currently on medical leave. She was an alcoholic and addicted to prescription drugs after suffering a leg injury in a motor vehicle accident a decade ago. The patient continued to have a PEG for tube feedings even though she was eating by mouth. I did not see her the first day because she was sleeping soundly and I could not arouse her. She was receiving cognitive language and dysphagia therapy.

In the first session, she did not describe any plans or desires once discharged even when cued with questions. I explained the Polyvagal Theory to her and then shared how touching the neck, yawning, and doing other exercises stimulate the vagus nerve to enhance rapport. I mentioned how rapport is important for focus and attention. I shared how the yawn stimulates the precuneus, which has responsibility for imagination and planning. I gave her several exercises to do on her own.

Therapy was cancelled the second day due to plans to remove the PEG. When I went in to check on her in the afternoon, she was crying because the PEG had not been removed because she had been sleeping heavily. I called for the nurse, who came and explained that the PEG removal had been postponed because she had not eaten her breakfast and had missed other meals as well due to sleeping. She expressed anger and frustration over the "unfairness" of it all. I re-explained the medical rationale that the nurse had provided, and the nurse assured her that the PEG would be removed if she ate.

She continued to express frustration, so I re-opened the topic about the vagus nerve system. I talked about alcohol dependency from the physiological perspective of the Polyvagal Theory. I suggested that an individual's body could become dependent on prescription drugs and alcohol to manage pain after being injured in an accident. Now that her body had withdrawn from alcohol, I suggested that exercises to tone the ventral vagus nerve could be used to experience the natural state of rapport, which might assist in clearer thinking and improved insight.

When I saw her the next afternoon, the PEG had been removed and she was smiling. She shared her plan for returning to work and to seek assistance for her alcoholism. Her ideas were optimistic and reasonable. She left the next day AMA (against medical advice) with her partner of fifteen years. While leaving AMA could be perceived as poor rapport, from a speech language pathology perspective she was eating for nutrition and had demonstrated functional abilities to make plans for the future. She had told me that she was going to make an appointment with a counselor.

5) A man in his sixties suffered a perforated duodenal ulcer, which caused perforation of the stomach and jejunum separation and required surgery. He suffered from acute respiratory failure and had to be intubated on two occasions, which caused vocal fold bowing. He had chemotherapy induced neuropathy, multiple myeloma, dysphagia, and feedings via a PEG. Voice quality was harsh and breathy with poor volume and decreased pitch range. His cough was weak.

In the first session, I instructed him in traditional vocal adduction exercises, breathing exercises for coordination of breath support with phonation, and the Valsalva maneuver. Participation was low, and there was as minimal change in voice. Then, I told him about the Polyvagal Theory and the theory of using nonverbal language behaviors to activate the ventral vagus nerve system for enhanced rapport. He participated in vagus nerve activation exercises.

I began by gently pressing his toes in the tiptoe position. Then I instructed him to look to the right and hold it until a sigh or yawn, and then look to the left and do the same. I moved to his neck and gently pressed on both sides just above the clavicle. Then I cupped my hands behind his ears. I instructed him in doing a long sniff and then prolonged "m" as if having smelled something delightful. Rapport had been established. Once again I instructed him in vocal adduction exercises and his voice was immediately much stronger. His eyes lit up with surprise. He said he had had a deep baritone voice, and this was the closest to it that he had heard since he had become ill.

The following day, he was able to recall three vagus nerve stimulation strategies that he had used. He could not recall the specific swallow strategies. By the end of the session his voice was louder and deeper when saying three-syllables words. His voluntary cough for airway protection was stronger. I noticed that his body became highly relaxed while producing the sniff and long "mmm" phonation.

The third session was limited in time due to his pain from constipation. Nursing was called. I mentioned that inhalations increase heart rate and exhalations decreases it. I related this to the sniff and prolonged hum technique. I reminded him that the sniff and hum had enabled him to become very relaxed the day before. I also had him experiment with touching his thumb to his index and middle fingers (vagus nerve activation) rather than making a fist (fight/flight). He shared that the techniques helped somewhat with pain management but did not substitute for pain medication. When the nurse arrived he described his pain with a clearer voice at a baritone pitch level. He was in rapport with the nurse.

6) A man in his forties was "found down" with a Glasgow Coma Scale of 6. He had suffered a large right cerebellar bleed with upward and downward herniation. He underwent a suboccipital craniectomy. He had acute respiratory failure, initially requiring a tracheostomy and mechanical ventilation. His tracheostomy was now capped. He had language of confusion, poor insight into deficits, inconsistent audible voice, poor pacing of speech, dysphagia, and gross motor ataxia. He had a PEG for all nutrition. He had difficulty imitating nonverbal behaviors to stimulate the vagus nerve due to poor coordination. Mouth opening for the yawn was limited and he did not maintain a gaze to the right or left.

The patient's parents were at the bedside, and I explained the Polyvagal Theory and how nonverbal language behaviors may activate the ventral vagus nerve to enhance rapport. I suggested nonverbal behaviors that they could practice with their son, with each other, and alone to promote a sense of greater rapport during this difficult time. I instructed them in how to do tactile stimulation of the neck, behind the ears, and on the feet of the patient. The next day the father showed me how he was standing on tiptoe and touching his own neck and behind his ears. He said that applying the exercises to himself helped him feel better. We had rapport.

During that session, the patient's sister was very angry and criticized care. She confronted me as to why her brother could not eat now that he had passed his swallow evaluation. She said she had searched swallow evaluations on the Internet that said passing meant the individual could eat food. I used several nonverbal language vagus nerve activation behaviors on myself and remained in authentic rapport as I explained the difference between a swallow evaluation with food and one for ice chips. I explained to her about the Polyvagal Theory and how important it is to keep the patient calm by those around him maintaining rapport. I suggested that by using specific natural nonverbal language behaviors she could exercise the ventral vagus nerve in a way that might help her feel calmer. She nodded "yes" while still crying.

The patient turned onto his side and asked for his back to be rubbed. I demonstrated how stroking gently up and down the backbone has an effect similar as to when the ventral vagus nerve is activated. His sister stroked his back in the same way and he became very calm and closed his eyes. Then he rolled onto his back and I had him clap his hands. He was unable to imitate the beat. I demonstrated to the sister and his parents how to engage him in hand clapping to music. I explained that music is theorized to stimulate the ventral vagus nerve and clapping is often done as part of engaging with music as well as engaging socially with others. I also explained that speaking and even the swallow involves rhythm. He was able to follow directions and imitate a 1-2 beat without assistance by the time I left, and the family was pleased with the session. I heard that he was decannulated three days later.

7) A woman in her sixties was admitted for chronic respiratory failure. She has been admitted frequently to the acute hospital for chronic obstructive pulmonary disease. She suffered from anxiety and chronic methadone dependence. She was using a nasal cannula for added oxygen. The patient had an intermittent guttural dysphonia due to a long-term vocal fold dysfunction. The best means of verbalizing was a gentle whisper, which was clearer than the dysphonia. However, she had a habit of forcing her voice and producing the dysphonia even when speaking slowly. Producing the whisper required verbal and visual cues.

I explained the Polyvagal Theory and demonstrated nonverbal behaviors that, very likely, activate the vagus nerve system. The patient was able to do the behaviors with minimal cues after instruction. The clarity of the whisper improved and the intermittent dysphonia decreased during the structured task of imitation without additional cues. The patient had become more socially engaged.

When I returned the next day, the patient could recall two out of the four nonverbal language activities. She could not recall any voice facilitation techniques but the clarity of her whisper was better. Her daughter was present and wanted to know how to help her mother speak more clearly. I explained what I told the patient about the Polyvagal theory and nonverbal behaviors. I had the daughter imitate some of the behaviors and report on whether there was a change in her sense of rapport. She reported that she felt more comfortable and relaxed after doing them. She was excited to encourage her mother to do a few of them before the other exercises, especially after hearing the clear whisper.

On the third visit, that patient shared that she was feeling anxious. Her voice was forced and dysphonic. I suggested she "warm up" doing the nonverbal behaviors I had taught her. I then reminded her to whisper. She produced the whisper in three syllable utterances in response to questions. She did not need visual or verbal cues for structured trials. While voice was dysphonic for spontaneous speech, the patient had made good gains. Rapport had been maintained.

8) A woman in her sixties suffered an aneurysm of the left segment of the middle communicating cerebral artery. This resulted in respiratory failure requiring a tracheostomy and mechanical ventilation. She was now using a t-piece and was on oxygen. She had tolerated a Passy Muir Valve (PMV) with minimal voicing prior to a decline in condition. She had been discharged from speech therapy due to inability to progress.

Her medical status was now stable and she was ready to begin using the PMV again. She was unable to vocalize but answered simple abstract yes/no questions with slight head gestures. Facial expressions were minimal yet appropriate. Family members were at her bedside daily. Her hands were in restraints when she was unsupervised because she would pull at her trache. Her ability to follow gross motor commands was poor.

I explained the Polyvagal Theory to the patient and family and how certain nonverbal language behaviors enhance rapport. The daughter became very excited and motivated after receiving the information. I instructed her in some basic nonverbal language exercises, including gently pushing the toes towards the nose to emulate tiptoe, a posture that often goes with enhanced focus towards a goal (like reaching or searching).

I began the next session with the same exercises to stimulate the vagus nerve pathways. By the end of the session the patient's range of motion for the head nod and shake had increased. Also, greater motor movement was produced to push back against my hand with her feet and when she attempted to pull herself forward when I took her hands.

During the third and final session of that week (Friday), the patient eyes opened wider when she was addressed, and facial expression had increase a bit more in range of motion. The patient was still unable to vocalize but the cough was louder. The daughter was very excited to have the nonverbal exercises. I went back for a day later the following week. The daughter saw me in the corridor and came out of the room. She said, "I thought I'd let you know that Mom's restraints were removed last week. We are so grateful and excited to see her spirits soar." It makes great sense that this is what happens, even metaphorically, when clinicians, clients, and families are in the state of authentic rapport.

Sixteen

CONSIDERATIONS FOR FUTURE EXPLORATION

"Life is change, and the brain is the device for recording changes—for forming memories through learning."   Joseph LeDoux (2002:134)

One purpose for this guidebook is to inspire your imagination regarding clinical application, further exploration, and formal research. This includes 1) the role of the theory of Nonverbal Language Integration in naturally activating the vagus nerve system to enhance learning outcomes through authentic rapport; 2) ways to assess this system; 3) ways to simulate this system; 4) the direct results of the exercises on other motor abilities; and 5) the individuals and the variety of health, learning, and behavioral issues that can benefit. What I know for sure is that this journey of exploration since July 2018 has done more than inspire me to continue investigating the vagus nerve. The results have changed how I do therapy, my interactions with others, and how I live my own life.

I did not have to pass my blood pressure test at the medical office to confirm that certain nonverbal language exercises have a positive effect on rapport and, very likely, on outcomes. My ability to concentrate, do research, recall the content, ride in a car with significantly decreased unnecessary reactions, and my overall comfort in noisy environments has improved. However, I am happy to report that in May 2019 I did pass my blood pressure test at the medical office (137/84) in spite of feeling quite anxious while it was being taken. This indicates that my physiological system has learned something.

My grandchildren have shown continued in interest in the vagus nerve, and they are the ones who encouraged me to write this all down in a guidebook for them. They asked if I had put their names in it when they found out that I was close to being finished. At that time Kerrigan was nine, Gregor was seven, and Conrad was five. My daughter, Elise, who has an elementary school teaching credential, recently shared an observation. She said that Gregor and Conrad got into a heated verbal fight and told each other they never wanted to play together again. Then, in less than a minute, they apologized to each other without any intervention by her.

A week later, I was watching Gregor and Conrad play a video game together on my iPad. Gregor got very upset at something Conrad did and they both ended up yelling at each other. I told them to sit on the couch side by side, which they did reluctantly. Like I have done in the midst of previous heated arguments, I told them to look at each other from the side until they sighed or yawned. Gregor attempted to explain the reason why he got upset. I did not allow dialogue, and told them to do it again. Then I told them both to put their hands on their own necks. Again Gregor attempted to provide an excuse for his angry reaction. I told them to try to yawn in each other's faces. After attempting that, they began to laugh and wanted to resume the game. Only then did I share my viewpoint about allowing a device to provoke their anger towards each other, and they spontaneously gave each other a hug. They had reestablished rapport.

The theory of Nonverbal Language Integration explains how nonverbal language behaviors activate the ventral vagus nerve pathways for homeostasis, which enhances rapport. Moore (2006) discusses rapport in relationship to empathy, and it's influence on outcomes. "Understanding empathy could facilitate the rapport building stage in initiating the therapeutic process, maximizing personal interactions with others and facilitating the development of diagnostic and treatment materials" (Moore, 2006:20). It has already been established that ventral vagus nerve activation for social engagement is required for empathy.

This theory has the potential to inspire research within a variety of areas where physiological and overt behaviors are amenable to intervention or enrichment. It could be researched in regard to health and wellness, rehabilitation, social engagement (including sexuality), sensory integration, and even education. Rapport is important to optimize learning, which is an essential component of adaptation. "Life is change, and the brain is the device for recording changes—for forming memories through learning" (LeDoux (2002:134).

While completing this guidebook, I realized that the Theory of Nonverbal Language Integration has helped me to better understand recovery from grief as well. Sobbing produces that familiar tension in the neck. Yet, while grieving is also an area for abundant research, it is beyond the scope of this guidebook. It was time to end this guidebook in order to bring forth this introductory information.

Chuck watches the financial news every morning, so I often listen for tidbits of applicable information while I write. My attention was drawn to comments being made about Oreo cookies. The captions said the interviewee was Dirk Van De Put, CEO of Mondelez, which is the company that makes Oreo cookies. He said that staying playful and doing things enjoyable are important, yet they need to be "in line" with each other's expectations. "When we go too far and do something that is unacceptable, we need to readjust and adapt to the other individual's taste." Van De Put said it can be a challenge to keep the complexity managed and supply the information in an efficient and effective way." This CEO's advice about Oreo cookies fits well with what I had read in *Vagotonia* by Eppinger and Hess, those early researchers of the vagus nerve. "A detailed review of the literature cannot be provided here owing to the great abundance of the facts" (Eppinger and Hess, 1915:5).

I realized that this is what I have attempted to do. This guidebook is my attempt to share a discovery and a new theory in a professional and scientific way that includes just enough facts. This means it must comply with the standards of the American Speech-Language-Hearing Association and the Center for Medicare Services in regard to evidenced based practices and reporting. Also, while a significant amount of content is complex, I have attempted to make it as engaging as possible by interweaving my personal story. It shares the basics of what I have discovered and learned from researching the vagus nerve since discovering the Q Collar in July 2018 and how I, ultimately, settled on the theory of Nonverbal Language Integration

As I mentioned, this information opens up endless avenues for literature research, personal exploration, and formal scientific research. This is what I continue to do and the results are exciting. Yet this guidebook is not the place to share these findings. What I do know is that I now have a passion for investigating the effects of integrating the theory of Nonverbal Language Integration into my daily practices. It is my belief that nonverbal language exercises that tone the vagus nerve system do more than enhance rapport. Understanding and exercising this system of equilibrium promote a sense of wellbeing.

Just before completing this guidebook, I had the opportunity to work a full day at the hospital. One patient has been there for many years. A neck fracture resulted in quadriplegia. He had a lifelong tracheostomy and chronic respiratory services are required. He had just recovered from an illness, and was downgraded from eating regular food consistencies. He could speak clearly over the trache. He told me that it felt like the "whole swallowing area has shortened," so he only wanted pureed foods

Before writing this guidebook, I would have focused therapy on teaching the traditional swallowing exercises and airway protection strategies during trial feedings of food. Now, in addition to those exercises and strategies, I added information on the vagus nerve and my findings regarding Nonverbal Language Integration. He replied that he could feel his body from the inside. I confirmed his observation because the vagus nerve does not travel through the spinal column.

I said that in 1915, physicians identified that nerves commingle and that fibers from the vagus nerve even co-mingle with the pelvic nerves and go to the genitals.

This means sensual pleasure can be derived from the imagination. "I know," he said almost secretively. I guided him in the progressive vagus nerve exercise. His swallow became louder. I then did traditional swallowing therapy instruction. At the end of the session he said that the swallow did not "feel shortened" anymore and that it felt stronger. He also noticed that his voice sounded stronger. He had a smile on his face when I left. I knew that the vagus nerve has efferent laryngeal branches important for voice and the swallow. I documented functional progress with his swallow. Yet, the direct affects of exercising the sensory vagus nerve on the motor functions of the laryngeal nerve is an important area to research.

A timely article came out in ASHA's publications after I had written the first draft of this guidebook. It was about using advances in neuroplasticity to improve outcomes in neurogenic communication disorders (Hengst et al., 2019). It was a rich review of the research literature that shows the relationships that exists between animal and human research on neuroplasticity and environmental enrichments. The review was done to "identify opportunities that will lead to improved outcomes for individuals with neurogenic communication disorders" (Hengst et al., 2019:217). In regard to research with humans, "it is critical to recognize the importance of voluntary activities (where opportunities exist for participants to engage in personally relevant and meaningful activities) and to recognize the need to optimize the experiential quality of communication for specific individual, in specific settings, at specific times" (Hengst et al., 2019:219).

This is another way to think about Nonverbal Language Integration exercises that activate the vagus nerve. There are interrelationships between 1) the sympathetic and parasympathetic nervous systems and 2) the ventral vagus nerve and postures, gestures, and facial expressions in many vertebrates. The difference with humans is that people can activate nonverbal communication behaviors voluntarily in personally meaningful ways to optimize rapport with different people in various settings. While this guidebook does not cover the variety of types of communication settings, what Hengst et al. (2019:220) reminds us is that communication "interactions are always situated in sociocultural activities."

Porges calls the ventral vagus nerve the system of social engagement. The theory of Nonverbal Language Integration identifies specific nonverbal language behaviors as innate automatic actions that reset the ventral vagus nerve for interpersonal communication and optimal rapport. The theory shows how exercising these behaviors voluntarily tones the ventral vagus nerve pathways. I have followed ASHA guidelines regarding responsible conduct of research and reporting specified by Minifie et al. (2011) to develop this theory. Yet, this guidebook had to go through one more process before making it available to clinicians. It was important to me that it be peer reviewed according to ASHA's Peer Review Procedures.

Seventeen

THE PEER REVIEW

The American Speech-Language-Hearing Association (ASHA) has set peer review procedures and guidelines primarily for research articles being submitted for publication in one of its journals (ASHA, Peer Review Procedures, n.d.). According to ASHA, there are two goals when reviewing work that is submitted for publication. One is to evaluate the merit of the work and the other goal is to offer critiques that improve the manuscript. Reviewers use an established reporting framework in order to evaluate the content with consistency. Generally, independent researchers within the same field of research are selected to be reviewers.

Debbie Love-Sudduth, M.A, CCC-SLP, agreed to do the work entailed for a peer review. Prior to becoming an SLP, she had been a high school math teacher. She had also worked in information systems (IS). I decided that the areas of focus for journal submissions could also be applied to this guidebook. I did my best to adhere to evidence-based practice guidelines while developing the theory of Nonverbal Language Integration for activating the ventral vagus nerve and the exercises that tone it. Therefore, I used ASHA's peer review guidelines to create a questionnaire for the review.

The questionnaire is as follows:

Thank you for your generous offer to review *Nonverbal Language Integration for Exercising Vagus Nerve Pathways*. In order to assist you with the process, I have drawn upon Peer Review Procedures by the American Speech-Language-Hearing Association to create this feedback questionnaire. It is my hope that you will read this manuscript as if you yourself were the author. This book is intended to serve as a guide that informs other clinicians about the vagus nerve pathways and behaviors that can exercise it. The purpose of this work is also to motivate others to explore how Nonverbal Language Integration concepts and exercises can be used to enhance rapport and outcomes within their practices.

The format of blending personal story with the review of the scientific literature serves to show how the theory evolved as well as adding to the ease of reading. It is my hope that you find the knowledge gained from reviewing this manuscript makes the time and effort dedicated to this voluntary review process worthwhile.

Please circle yes or no and provide one sentence regarding the rationale for your answer.

1. Is the logic behind the inspiration and development of the Theory of Nonverbal Language Integration consistent?   Yes   No

2. Is each hypothesis clearly stated, including the final hypothesis? Yes   No

3. Are the reasons for developing new hypotheses clear?   Yes   No

4. Is the development of the Theory of Nonverbal Language Integration motivated by reliable literature review? Yes   No

5. Are interpretations of the professional literature clear?   Yes   No

6. Does the creation of the Theory of Nonverbal Language Integration belong within the knowledge base of a speech-language pathologist?   Yes   No

7. Is the rationale for creating this guidebook adequate?   Yes   No

8. Is the literature review sufficient in regard to scope?   Yes   No

9. Is the guidebook organized in a way that enhances understanding of the material and the creation of the theory?   Yes   No

10. Is the content clear?   Yes   No

11. Have the subjective research, literature review, and case examples shown the information and exercises to have clinical significance for other healthcare or educational intervention disciplines?   Yes   No

12. Does the Theory of Nonverbal Integration for Exercising Vagus Nerve Pathways have personal significance?   Yes   No

Are there any additional comments?

It was a challenge to wait over a month for the review, because it was very easy for doubts to set in. Yet, I continued to teach about the vagus nerve and the exercises that most likely activated it. Each time I was called to work at the hospital, I observed how the affects on establishing rapport with patients and families were positive. I continued to use my grandchildren and myself for subjective research. My additional findings and comments by a Jungian analyst are included in the Epilogue.

Then on July 18, 2019 an email arrived alerting me that a reviewer had mailed the feedback questionnaire. Speech-language pathologist Debbie Love-Sudduth wrote, "I was engrossed in your manuscript. It flowed so well, made so much sense and was very clear, logical and sounds like an effective and necessary treatment. In fact, we do some of the exercises frequently on our own. Thank you for including me!"

When her questionnaire arrived, the answers to all 12 questions were "yes." The comments are as follows:

1. Logic is explained and augmented by real life examples from experiments involving adults and children.

2. Interim hypotheses were clearly stated and explained using research in each instance.

3. Personal explanations and observations were enlightening and comical, which drew attention to their impact.

4. Literature cited is appropriate to support each incremental step of the process.

5. Each step is documented using applicable examples and clear language explanations.

6. The explanations paired with real-life exercises accompanying them were very clear.

7. Absolutely! This fits within the scope of a SLP's practice. Currently, many SLPs use some of these methods.

8. This is demonstrated clearly on the front end and backed by real-time exercises on the back end.

9. Yes, the author used the combination of experience and literature to effectively define the NLI theory.

10. An SLP could take this manual and use the NLI in practice due to the examples provided and SLP knowledge. I would attend a workshop!

11. Using the examples provided as a platform, I believe the teaching profession can use the behaviors for calming. I found myself experiencing similar results that were described when applying it to my person.

12. Dorothy Bohntinsky has been my mentor for more than eight years, and continually provides expert advice to me and to her patients in order to make them more effective and enriched in their daily lives.

EPILOGUE

From Golf to Innate Releasing Mechanisms

All those factors, therefore, that were essential to our near and remote ancestors will be essential to us, for they are embedded in the inherited organic system.
Carl Gustav Jung (Stevens, 1994/2001:51)

It was now early July 2019, and Chuck and I were once again on vacation at South Lake Tahoe. A year had passed since I first read about the Q Collar being used to prevent concussion in football. Chuck and I had been practicing the progressive vagus nerve exercise (pages 92-93) for a couple of weeks. I, of course, had been exploring, exercising, and writing about the vagus nerve for a year. I had been sharing Nonverbal Language Integration with inpatients for several months.

Since we had been coming to the same place in South Lake Tahoe a couple of times a year since 2000, it had become a "natural environment" for observing any changes in my mood and behavior. The first difference that I noticed immediately was golfing. We usually play golf four times at a municipal golf course during each vacation. We had not played golf since September 2018. I have been known to get so frustrated while trying to get to the green that I would finally pick my ball up and refuse to putt. This did not happen once during our first round of golf, and I wondered if my game had actually improved. I used various nonverbal language behaviors to activate my vagus nerve while walking to the ball. Most importantly, I not only putted every hole, but my ball was in the hole in two to three putts.

My game deteriorated the second day, which seems to always happen to me after a good round. The difference is that my expressions of frustration only lasted momentarily. My mood heightened each time I reminded myself to use one of the nonverbal language behaviors that "resets" the autonomic system back to homeostasis. Again, I made many of the holes in two putts once I got on the green.

The third day was much better, and my game was more consistent again. I noticed a significant shift when we walked towards the sixth hole. I stopped thinking about my swing and focused on walking differently on the course. I walked heel to toe and pushed off with my toes keeping the concept of being on tiptoe in mind. I also widened my nostrils and took in slow deep inhalations. The

113

eighth and ninth par-three holes, which once had long wide-open fairways, were now narrow with boggy hazards to hit over due to storm waters having changed the course. Last year I refused to hit from those tees, not wanting to get frustrated over losing a ball. The difference was that I was not only still in good humor while walking towards those holes, I smiled at my reluctance to lose a ball. I hit over the boggy hazard on the eighth hole. And surprisingly, I not only hit over the hazard on the ninth hole, I finished the hole in four strokes. That was a first.

Now, as expected, the fourth day of golf was worse than the third. The main issue was that while the ball went fairly straight, it did not go as far. In the past, taking stroke after stroke to get the ball up the fairway or out of the rough would have caused frustration to build within me. The course was also more crowded and noisy. Ordinarily, I would have picked up my ball and, maybe, even refused to putt. However, I persevered with good humor. Again, the most surprising shift in experience was that I hit over both hazards and finished the eighth and ninth holes in four strokes.

While I cannot state that toning the ventral vagus nerve improves the ability to play golf, what I did observe is that it made the game more enjoyable to me. In the past, I would confess that I did not really enjoy the sport. For over two decades, I played in order for Chuck to enjoy playing the game. I played for exercise because we always walk the courses. The game itself could often cause me to become frustrated, which was something I had to work at constantly.

Golf requires mental discipline to avoid distracting thoughts and to focus on the immediate environment. It requires heightened attention to sensations in the body in order to determine footing and make the necessary adjustments. It requires the analysis of distance in order to select the correct club. It requires attention to body posture and the kinesiology of the swing from the back swing to follow through. It requires the ability to tune out physical distractions from the loud voices of other players to water hazards. In the past, this may have been so challenging that it caused the game to be more like work than play. I can now say that toning my ventral vagus nerve has helped me to have more fun playing the game of golf; it no longer seemed like work. I realized that my experience with golf took me full circle to the article I read about the Q Collar one year ago. Reporter Danni Washington (Washington, n.d.) observed that her ability to do a mental/physical task improved immediately when wearing the Q Collar.

The next difference that I noticed was dining. We took a two-day side trip to Reno to celebrate Chuck's birthday. We both enjoy the El Dorado buffet, but I often become nervous over the table location because of the noisy stations where dirty plates are stacked. I decided to see what happened when we were offered a booth near such an area. While this was not something I would seek out, I realized that I felt very relaxed throughout the meal. This happened twice, and I noticed a significant positive shift in my mood around clattering plates and silverware. The clanging made me shudder in the past, and I attributed it to having excellent hearing. I now realized that my reactions had been caused by an over reactive autonomic sympathetic nervous system. Based on these observations, I continue to be confidant that the ventral vagus nerve can be exercised directly through nonverbal language behaviors. The result is an enhanced overall functioning of the parasympathetic nervous system.

Most importantly, I have begun to view challenges from a very different perspective. I had not considered that I had a problem with my "nervous system" when it came to being bothered by noises or becoming frustrated over my performance in golf. It was my "normal," and I attributed my difficulties to physical challenges (hearing being too good, arms being too short for good distance in golf, or "white coat" anxiety in terms of blood pressure). Yet, it was not until these difficulties significantly resolved after toning the ventral vagus nerve through nonverbal language exercises that I realized that many of my "challenges" had been due to some kind of over activity of my autonomic nervous system.

I became even more confident about Nonverbal Language Integration from an innate perspective after reading a small book about Carl Gustavo Jung's work, which I brought with me on this vacation. I decided to acquire *Jung: A Very Short Introduction* by Anthony Stevens (1994/2001) after reconnecting with Jungian analyst Wynette Barton. Barton and I were not only classmates and graduated together from Wisdom University in 2006, she was the peer reviewer for my doctoral dissertation. Barton first career was as an SLP before becoming a Diplomate Analyst, C.G. Jung Institute Zurich. She was excited to read the manuscript of this guidebook, so I decided to study Jung while waiting for Love-Sudduth's peer review to be completed. Barton's initial response was that she loved it.

Stevens (1994:51) quoted a piece from *The Collected Works of C.G. Jung, VIII:* "All those factors, therefore, that were essential to our near and remote ancestors will be essential to us, for they are embedded in the inherited organic system." Stevens then writes, "Very similar ideas to Jung's have become current . . . in the relatively new science of ethology (that branch of behavioral biology which studies animals in their natural habitats)." He went on to explain how ethnologists have identified "innate releasing mechanisms, or IRMs" as a "behavior repertoire" that is "built into the central nervous system of the species."

IRMs are released by when a "sign stimulus" occurs. A characteristic "pattern of behaviors" evolves to ensure adaptation to the situation. Stevens uses the green head of the mallard duck being the sign stimulus for courtship as an example. He then addressed how Jung did not categorized archetypes to be "an inherited idea" but, instead, to be "an inherited mode of functioning" (Stevens, 1994:52). This could also be applied to specific nonverbal behaviors, which may have evolved into a sophisticated set of IRMs. For each individual, a subset of nonverbal language IRMs could become a person's personal repertoire of pragmatics (body, facial, and vocal expressions). In this way, individualized pragmatics is integrated as sign stimuli to make the necessary adjustments for successful social engagement, rapport, and performance.

Stevens (1994:71) uses the term "syzygy" to represent archetypical opposites that exist unconsciously in each individual. I researched the word, and in medicine, syzygy refers to the yoking together of organs without loss of specific identity. In astronomy, it refers to the linear alignment of celestial bodies, such as the sun, earth, and moon during an eclipse. I realized that in neurophysiology, the dorsal vagus nerve, sympathetic nervous system, and ventral vagus nerve can be considered to have syzygy as well. They have a similar form of linear alignment when viewed as innate reactivity that happens unconsciously in each individual.

It takes practice to put awareness of the "syzygy" nature of the three pathways of innervation within the autonomic nervous system into our consciousness and into our bodies. When something startling happens, the first unconscious behavior is often immobilization triggered by the dorsal vagus nerve. It is as if one is frozen in place in order for the senses to analyze the threat. Then, the sympathetic nervous is triggered to prepare for and activate the fight/flight response. However, when there is no immediate threat to survival, those preparatory behaviors, very likely, activate the ventral vagus nerve and reset the system to homeostasis.

According to Stevens (1994:72) Jung "borrowed" the term homeostasis from biology and applied it to human psychology. "Homeostasis is the means by which all organic systems keep themselves in a state of balance, despite changes in the environment." This applies on the levels of molecules to our planet as a whole, each having a system of "self-regulation. . . . Jung held that the laws which prevail in the cosmos must also prevail in the psyche." This means that self-regulation through jugular vein compression and omohyoid muscle innervation it can also be nature's way of activating homeostasis within all animals that have a vertebrae. The body's reaction not only creates a physical change to prevent slosh in the brain, it also activates the neurological pathways that enhance rapport and even performance. The difference with humans is that self-regulation can be brought to a conscious level and activated voluntarily through specific nonverbal behaviors.

The theory of Nonverbal Language Integration blends the basic ideas of the Polyvagal Theory and pragmatics (nonverbal language behaviors) to utilize the concepts in a different way. It brings forth to a conscious level the behaviors of self-regulation that are already happening on a subconscious level to make sure that things do not get worse. While the theory of Nonverbal Language Integration could be considered to be a universal paradigm, personal differences (or IRM repertoires) are respected and encouraged. Each individual can do the nonverbal movements without concerns regarding accuracy. The results can actually create surprises that individuals do not usually get with "interventions" that rely primarily on discussion or stimulus/response instruction.

Nonverbal language behaviors become "tools" that actually produce contemporary feelings of homeostasis. These "tools" exercise the bidirectional pathways of communication that already exist between the brain and the body for promoting optimal responses. The body's natural way of freeing emotions from previous concerns and fears is harnessed to re-establish rapport. Within this state, productive and helpful insights are inspired when something challenging happens. With exercise, these bidirectional pathways of communication are toned, rapport is maintained for longer periods, and enduring outcomes result through neuroplasticity.

Each individual can learn to observe progression in activating optimal self-regulating responses when threats are perceived. Instead of unconsciously reacting with nonverbal behaviors to a "sign stimulus" in order to recover from negative dynamics, one can learn to use challenges as opportunities to use nonverbal language behaviors as tools for enhancing rapport, awareness, focus, and responses. In conflicts, it moves the individual beyond a truce and actually ends the "war," whether with oneself or with others. Instead of abiding in distancing disagreements, these "tools" can actually help establish rapport. The individuals involved can rethink the situation in a way that helps everyone feel better after triggering the ventral vagus nerve.

In practice, turbulent feelings can be used as warning signs. Instead of panicking or emotions flaring up, the body and face is moved consciously in ways that return the autonomic system nervous to equilibrium quickly. In time, the ventral vagus nerve is toned and reactivity declines. All involved benefit from the evolving positive adjustments, and the progress with rapport promotes optimism in being able to respond to uncertainties with greater calmness and more careful judgment.

When specific IRMs that elevate mood are voluntarily activated through the natural and innate tools identified within the theory of Nonverbal Language Integration, the best strategies of communication can be employed to serve others and ourselves better. Instead of trading tensions, which can weigh upon one's outlook and can cause conflicts to escalate, interactions are quickly mediated in ways that promote greater satisfaction among others and within oneself. While we may not be able to prevent problems from happening, we do have the ability to improve how our body (emotionally, physically, mentally, and spiritually) responds to triggers that exist along internal and external continuums of mental uncertainties and unpleasant environmental stimuli. Instead of reacting in ways that can inflate tensions, the ventral vagus nerve can be toned to create new habits for optimal self-regulatory responses that promote a more stable equilibrium for rapport while also respecting individual differences.

The theory of Nonverbal Language Integration stresses an outlook that is forward thinking and actually raises our spirits. Feelings, emotions, and specific nonverbal language behaviors become tools that serve a very important role in helping us look at our personal assets in ways that can be used to create solutions. Instead of being immobilized or rushing ahead, we can use "negative" reactions to alert us that an opportunity has arisen to activate the ventral vagus nerve. We can take a moment to pause, step back from toe to heel, rise up upon tiptoe, stretch, and gently touch the neck in order for insights to become almost amazingly accessible. In this way, we are consciously using IRMs, our natural self-regulatory functions, to re-establish rapport. We are then ready to learn and adapt in ways that promote successful outcomes for personal adjustment and life-long growth.

Two months after writing this epilogue, Wynette Barton and I talked on the phone for about an hour about Nonverbal Language Integration. She had not seen the Epilogue, so I emailed it to her. She wrote back a couple of days later.

The Theory of Nonverbal Language Integration is stimulating and thought provoking. I especially like the way the guidebook blends your unique knowledge and skills with sound observation and research from the literature, showing how this theory was developed. It has applications to psychoanalysis in helping to develop rapport and in other ways that I am still exploring. Nonverbal Language Integration may have valuable applications in many fields and is definitely worthy of further attention, research, and development.

Just before publishing this guidebook, I asked my grandchildren about their favorite way to activate the vagus nerve when upset. Kerrigan said that she raises her toes towards her nose or goes on tiptoe. Gregor said that he puts his hand to his neck. Conrad (age five) said, "Grams, I do kegels. Nobody can see me doing that."

REFERENCES

American Speech-Language-Hearing Association. (2016). Code of Ethics. Retrieved from: https://www.asha.org/Code-of-Ethics/.

American Speech-Language-Hearing Association. (2016). Scope of Practice. Retrieved from: https://www.asha.org/policy/sp2016-00343/.

American Speech-Language-Hearing Association. Peer Review Procedures. Retrieved from: https://academy.pubs.asha.org/prep-the-asha-journals-peer-review-excellence-program/peer-review-procedures/.

Anderson, Raymond, D. (1989). Kierkegaard on Ethics in Communication with Self. In Charles V. Roberts and Kittie W. Watson (Eds.), *Intrapersonal Communication Processes: Original Essays*. New Orleans, LA: SPECTRA Incorporated, Publishers.

Andrew James, R. and Andrews, Mary. A. (2000). *Family-Based Treatment in Communication Disorders: A Systematic Approach* (Second Edition). DeCalb, IL: Janelle Publications, Inc.

Ansell, Barbara J. (1991). Slow-to-Recover Brain Injured Patients. *Journal of Speech, Language, and Hearing Research*. 34:1017-1022. Retrieved from: https://pubs.asha.org/doi/pdf/10.1044/jshr.3405.1017.

Apel, Ken and Self, Trisha. (2003). Evidence-Based Practice. *The ASHA Leader*. 8: 6-7. Retrieved from: https://leader.pubs.asha.org/doi/10.1044/leader.FTR1.08162003.6.

Apple, Charles, G. (1989). Freedom of Choice: Intrapersonal Communication and Emotion. In Charles V. Roberts and Kittie W. Watson (Eds.), *Intrapersonal Communication Processes: Original Essays*. New Orleans, LA: SPECTRA Incorporated, Publishers.

Barnlund, Dean C. (1973). Communication" The Context of Change. In C. David Mortensen (Ed.). *Basic Readings in Communication Theory*. San Francisco, CA: Harper and Row, Publishers.

Bohntinsky, Dorothy. (2016). *Transformational Healing through the Integration of Self.* Hayward, CA: In-Word Bound Publishing. (Published dissertation from 2006 D.Min.).

Boone, Daniel. (1971). *The Voice and Voice Therapy*. Englewood Cliffs, New Jersey: Prentice-Hall, Inc.

Boyle, Michael, Beita-Ell, Carolina, Milewski, Kathryn M., and Fearon, Alison. (2018). Self-Esteem, Self-Efficacy, and Social Support as Predictors of Communicative Participation in Adults Who Stutter. *American Journal of Speech, Language, and Hearing Research*, 61, 1893-1906. https://doi.org/10.1044/2018_JSLHR-S-17-0043.

Brasher, Valentina L. and McCance, Kathryn L. (2012). Structure and Function of the Cardiovascular and Lymphatic System. In S. Heuther and K. McCance (Eds.), Understanding Neurophysiology (Fifth Edition). St. Louis: MO: ELSEVIER MOSBY.

Cavanna, Andrea E. and Trimble, Michael R. (2006). The precuneus: a review of its functional anatomy and behavioral correlates. *Brain* (2006), 129, 564-583. https://doi.org/10.1093/brain/awl004.

CIAO – Career Improvement and Advancement Opportunities. Retrieved from: http://www.ciaoseminars.com/common/vitalstim_CourseCriteria.cfm.

Chowdhary, S. and Townsend J.N. Nitric oxide and hypertension: not just an endothelium derived relaxing factor! (2001) *Journal of Human Hypertension.* 15, 219-227. Retrieved from: http://www.lafranceagricole.fr/r/Publie/FA/p1/Infographies/Dossier/2013-06-14/69263_15.pdf.

Christensen, Stephanie and Wright, Heather Harris. (2014). Quantifying the Effort of Individuals with Aphasia Invest in Working Memory Tasks Through Heart Rate Variability. *American Journal of Speech Language Pathology*. 23, S361-S370. Retrieved from: https://pubs.asha.org/doi/10.1044/2014_AJSLP-13-0082.

Thomas, Clayton L (Ed.) (1973). *Taber's Encyclopedic Medical Dictionary*. Philadelphia. PA: F. A. Davis Company.

Collins, J.J., Lin, C.E., Berthoud, H.R., and Papka, R.E. (1999). Vagal afferents from the uterus and cervix provide direct connection to the brain stem. *Cell and Tissue Research*. 295, 43-54. https://www.researchgate.net/publication/13358596_Vagal_afferents_from_the_uterus_and_cervix_provide_direct_connection_to_the_brainstem.

Conte, Sergio, Wang, Fang, Sala, Nicoletta, Casciaro, Francesco Losito, Orsucci, Franco, Serafini, Giuseppe, Kaleagasioglu, Ferda, Mendolicchio, Leonardo, Norman, Rich, and Conte, Elio. (2017). The Transcutaneous Nerve Stimulation Output of the NUCam Device of Solace Lifesciences Is Found to Be a Multifractal and Therefore It Is Indicated in the Treatment of Heart Rate Variability in the Dysfunction of Autonomic Nervous System in Anxiety. *Journal of Behavioral and Brain Science*. 7, 532-543. Retrieved from: https://www.scirp.org/journal/PaperInformation.aspx?paperID=80458&.

Crossman, A.R. and Neary, D. (2015). *Neuroanatomy: An Illustrated Colour Text; Fifth Edition.* New York, New York: Churchill Livingstone Elsevier.

Cutter, Matthew. (2018). Chomp. Slurp. Smack. SNAP! *The ASHA Leader*. 23, 44-52. Retrieved from: https://leader.pubs.asha.org/doi/10.1044/leader.FTR1.23072018.44.

Darley, Frederick L., Aronson, Arnold E., Brown, Joe E. (1975). *Motor Speech Disorders*. Philadelphia, PA: W.B. Sanders Company.

DiCarlo, Louis M. (1974). Communication therapy for problems associated with cerebral palsy. In Stanley Dickensen (Ed.). *Communication Disorders: Remedial Principals and Practices* (357-397). Glenview, Illinois: Scott, Foresman and Company.

DiCesare, Christopher, Foss, Kim Barbara, Schneider, Daniel, Edward, Thomas, Staci, Schneider, Daniel, Edwards, Nicholas, and Myer, Gregory. (2017). The Effects of Jugular Compression Applied during High Intensity Power, Strength and Postural Control Tasks. *Thieme Medical Publishers,* New York, New York. Retrieved from http://q30innovations.com/wp-content/uploads/2018/02/6.-Dicesare-2017-CRC-The-Effects-of-External-Jugular-Compression-Applied.. ..pdf.

Eadie, Tanya, Yorkston, Kathryn, Klasner, Estelle, Dudgeon, Brian, Deitz, Jean, Baylor, Carolby, Miller, Robert, and Antmann, Dagmar. (2006). Measuring Communicative Participation: A Review of Self-Report Instruments in Speech-Language Pathology. *American Journal of Speech Language Pathology*. 15, 307-320. Retrieved from: https://doi.org/10.1044/1058-0360(2006/030).

Eisenberg, Rita B. (1970). The Organization of Auditory Behavior, *Journal of Speech and Hearing Research*, 1970, 459-461. Extracted from: https://pubs.asha.org/doi/pdf/10.1044/jshr.1303.453.

Eppinger, Hans and Hess, Leo. (1915). *Vagotonia: A Clinical Study in Vegetative Neurology*. Revised Edition. The Nervous and Mental Disease Publishing Company, New York, New York.

Ertekin, Cumhur and Aydogdu, Ibrahim. (2003). Neurophysiology of swallowing. *Clinical Neurophysiology*. 114, 2226-2244. Retrieved from: https://www.researchgate.net/publication/249008568_Neurophysiology_of_swallowing.

Ertekin, Cumhur, Bulbul, Nazli Gamze, Uludag, Irem Fatma, Tiftikcloglur, Bedile Irem, Arici, Sehnaz, and Gurgor, Nevin. (2015). The electrophysiological association of spontaneous yawning and swallowing. *Experimental Brain Research*. 223, 2073-80. Springer-Verlag Berlin Heidelberg. Retrieved from: https://www.researchgate.net/publication/275665657_Electrophysiological_association_of_spontaneous_yawning_and_swallowing.

Fisher, Joseph A., Duffin, James, Mikulis, David, Sobczyk. (2015). The effect of jugular vein compression on cerebral hemodynamics in healthy subjects. Retrieved from: http://q30innovations.com/wp-content/uploads/2015/07/The-Effect-of-Jugular-Vein-Compression.pdf.

Fogel, Alan. (2013). *Body Sense: The Science and Practice of Embodied Self-Awareness*. New York, NY: W.W. Norton & Company, Inc.

Franca, Lucas G. Souza, Miranda, Jose G. Vivas, Leite, Marco, Sharma, Niraj K., Walker, Matthew, Lemieux, Louis, and Wang, Yujiang. (2018). Fractal and Multifractal Properties of Electrographic Recording of Human Brain Activity: Toward Its Use as a Signal Feature for Machine Learning in Clinical Applications. *Frontiers in Physiology*. Published online 10 December 2018. Retrieved from: https://www.frontiersin.org/articles/10.3389/fphys.2018.01767/full.

Franco, Jessica, Davis, Barbara L., Davis, John L. (2013). Increasing Social Interaction Using Prelinguistic Milieu Teaching With Nonverbal School Children With Autism. *Journal of Speech-Language Pathology*. 22, 489-502. Retrieved from: https://pubs.asha.org/doi/full/10.1044/1058-0360%282012/10-0103%29.

Friel-Patti, Sandy. (1994). Commitment to Theory. *Journal of Speech Language Pathology*. 3, 30-34. Retrieved from: https://pubs.asha.org/doi/pdf/10.1044/1058-0360.0302.30.

Geller, Elaine and Foley, Gilbert M. (2009). Expanding the "Ports of Entry" for Speech-Language Pathologists: A Relational and Reflective Model for Clinical Practice. *American Journal of Speech Language Pathology*. Feb 2009: 18:4-21. https://doi.org/10.1044/1058-0360(2008/07-0054).

Giuliano, F., Rampin, O., Allard, J. (2002). Neurophysiology and Pharmacology of Female Genital Sexual Response. *Journal of Sex Marital Therapy*. 28, 101-21. Retrieved from: https://www.researchgate.net/publication/11464571_Neurophysiology_and_Pharmacology_of_Female_Genital_Sexual_Response.

Greenstein, Ben and Greenstein, Adam. (2000). *Color Atlas of Neuroscience: Neuroanatomy and Neurophysiology*. New York, New York: Thieme.

Gudmundsson, Garner. (2014). Intracranial Pressure and the Role of the Vagus Nerve: A Hypothesis. *World Journal of Neuroscience*. 4, 164-169. Retrieved from: https://www.scirp.org/html/10-1390177_45599.htm.

Habib, Safia and Ali, Asif. (2011). The Biochemistry of Nitric Oxide. Indian Journal of Clinical Biochemistry , 26:3-17. Retrieved from: https://www.academia.edu/10641832/Biochemistry_of_Nitric_Oxide.

Harper, Robert, Wiens, Arthur, and Matarazzo, Joseph, D. 1978. *Nonverbal Communication: The State of the Art.* New York, New York: John Wiley and Sons.

Helou, Leah B., Rosen, Clark, Wang, Wei, Abbott, Katherine Verdolini. (2018). Intrinsic Laryngeal Muscle Response to a Public Speech Preparation Stressor, *Journal of Speech Hearing Language Research*, 61, 1525-1543. Retrieved from: https://doi.org/10.1044/2018_JSLHR-S-17-0153.

Holland, Audrey L. (2007). *Counseling in Communication Disorders: A Wellness Approach.* San Diego, CA: Plural Publishing.

Huether, Sue and McCance, Kathryn (Ed.). (2012). *Understanding Pathophysiology.* (Fifth Edition). St. Louis: MO: ELSEVIER MOSBY. "Alternations in Cognitive Systems, Cerebral Hemodynamics, and Motor Function."

Humbert, Ianessa A. (2011). Stimulating Swallowing: Essential Central and Peripheral Nervous System Targets. *The Asha Leader.* 16, 10-13. Retrieved from: https://doi.org/10.1044/leader.FTR1.16092011.10.

Iacoboni, Marco. (2008). *Mirroring People: The New Science of How We Connect with Others.* New York: Farrar, Straus, and Giroux.

Kapit, Wynn and Elson, Lawrence M. (1993). *The Anatomy Coloring Book: Second Edition.* New York, New York: Harper Collins Publishers.

Kimiko, Abe, Sarah E. M. Weisz, Rachelle L. Dunn, Martina C. DiGioacchino, Jennifer A. Nyentap, Seta Stanbouly, Juile A. Theurer, Yves Bureau, Rebecca H. Affoo, Ruth E. Martin. (2015.) Occurrence of the Yawn and Swallow are Temporally Related. *Dysphagia.* 30, 57-56. Retrieved from: https://link.springer.com/article/10.1007%2Fs00455-014-9573-2.

King, Rella R. and Berger, Kenneth W. (1971). *Diagnostic Assessment and Counseling Techniques for Speech Pathologists and Audiologists.* Pittsburg, PA: Stanwax House, Inc.

Kleim, Jeffery and Jones, Theresa. (2008). Principals of Experience-Dependent Plasticity: Implications for Rehabilitation After Brain Damage. *Journal of Speech, Language, and Hearing Research.* 51, S225-S239. Retrieved from: https://doi.org/10.1044/1092-4388(2008/018).

Kok, Bethany E., Coffey, Kimberly A., Cohn, Michael A., Catalino, Lahnna I., Vacharkulksemsuk, Tanya, Algoe, Sara B., Brantley, Mary and Fredrickson, Barbara. (2013). How Positive Emotions Build Physical Health: Perceived Positive Social Connections Account for the Upward Spiral Between Positive Emotions and Vagal Tone. *Psychological Science*. 24, 1123-1132. Retrieved from: https://pdfs.semanticscholar.org/18ca/501857b420b7716aa71a2d0d118ca25837 90.pdf?_ga=2.159537341.1857147401.1556717251-847747019.1556717251.

Kurland, Jacquie, Pulvermuller, Friedemann, Silva, Niclole, Burke, Katherine, Andriannopoulus, Mary. (2012). Constrained Verses Unconstrained Intensive Language Therapy in Two Individuals With Chronic, Moderate-to-Severe Aphasia of Speech: Behavioral and fMRI Outcomes. *American Journal of Speech Language Pathology*. 21, S65-S87. Retrieved from: https://pubs.asha.org/doi/10.1044/1058-0360%282012/11-0113%29.

LeDoux, Joseph. (2002). *Synaptic Self*. New York, New York: Penguin Books.

Lemire, Joe. (2017). Brain Protecting Q-Collar Technology Spreads through Sports World. *Sport Techie*. Retrieved from: https://www.sporttechie.com/q-collar-bauer-neuroshield-concussion-prevention-canada-brad-keselowski/.

Loler J.M., Navaux M.A., Previnaire, J.G. (2018). Positive Sexuality in Men with Spinal Cord Injury. *Spinal Cord*. 56, 1199-1206. Retrieved from: https://www.ncbi.nlm.nih.gov/pubmed/29967449.

Martin, Ruth, E. (2009). Neuroplasticity and swallowing. *Dysphagia*. 24, 218-229. Abstract retrieved from: https://search.proquest.com/openview/aedcb10dea5742f464028129e7f3a1cb/1?pq -origsite=gscholar&cbl=31829.

McDonald, James D. and Carroll, Jennifer. (1992). A Social Partnership Model for Assessing Early Communication Development. Language, Speech, and Hearing Services in the Schools. *American Speech, Language, and Hearing Association*. 2, 113-124. Retrieved from: https://pubs.asha.org/doi/full/10.1044/0161-1461.2302.113.

Mehrabian, Albert. (1972). *Nonverbal Communication*. Chicago, Ill: Aldine·Atherton.

Minifie, Fred D., Robey, Randall R., Horner Jennifer, Ingham, Janis C., Lansing, Charissa, McCartney Manes H., Alldredge, Eham-Eid, Slater, Sarah C., and Moss, Sharon. (2011). Responsible Conduct of Research in Communication Sciences and Disorders: Faculty and Student Perceptions, *Journal of Speech, Language and Hearing Research*. 54, S363-393. Retrieved from: https://pubs.asha.org/doi/10.1044/1092-4388%282010/09-0262%29 It had to be peer reviewed.

Moisik, Scott Reid and Gick, Bryan. (2017). The Quantal Larynx: The Stable Regions of Laryngeal Biomechanics and Implications. *Journal of American Speech and Hearing Research*. 3, 540-560.Retrieved from: https://pubs.asha.org/doi/10.1044/2016_JSLHR-S-16-0019.

Moore, Lisa (2006). Empathy: A Clinician's Perspective. *The ASHA Leader*. 11:16-35. https://doi.org/10.1044/leader.FTR5.11102006.16.

Mortensen, David C. (1972). *Communication: The Study of Human Interaction*. San Francisco, CA: McGraw Hill Book Company.

Newberg, Andrew and Waldman, Mark. (2010). *How God Changes Your Brain: Breakthrough Findings from a Leading Neuroscientist*. New York: New York: Ballantine Books Trade Paperbacks.

Newberg, Andrew and Waldman, Mark. (2016). *How Enlightenment Changes Your Brain: The New Science of Transformation*. New York, NY: Penguin Random House, LLC.

Nicolosi, Lucille, Harryman, Elizabeth, Kresheck, Janet. (1978). *Terminology of Communication Disorders: Speech, Language, Hearing*. Baltimore, MD: Williams & Wilkins.

Palmer, John M. (1972). *Anatomy for Speech and Hearing*. New York, New York: Harper and Row, Publishers.

Pelletier, Cathy. (2002). Beyond the Tongue Map: Evaluating Tasted and Smell Perception. *The ASHA Leader*. 7, 6-20. Retrieved from: https://leader.pubs.asha.org/doi/10.1044/leader.FTR2.07192002.6.

Perkins, William H. (1971). *Speech Pathology: An Applied Behavioral Science*. St. Louis, MO: The C.V. Mosby Company.

Platek SM, Mohamed FB, Gallup GG Jr. (2005). Contagious Yawning and the Brain. *Brain Research Cognitive Brain Research*. 23, 448-52. Retrieved from: https://www.ncbi.nlm.nih.gov/pubmed/?term=Yawn+and+precuneus.

Pompon Rebecca Hunting, Amtmann, Dagmar, Bombardier, Charles, and Kendall, Diane. (2018). Modifying and Validating a Measure of Chronic Stress for People with Aphasia. *Journal of Speech, Language, and Hearing Research*. 61, 2934-2949. Retrieved from: https://pubs.asha.org/doi/full/10.1044/2018_JSLHR-L-18-0173.

Porges, Stephen W. (2017). *The Pocket Guide to the Polyvagal Theory: The Transformative Power of Feeling Safe*. W.W. Norton & Company, Inc.: New York, New York.

Porges, Stephen W. (2007). The Polyvagal Perspective. *Biological Psychology* 74, 116-143. Retrieved from: https://pdfs.semanticscholar.org/18ca/501857b420b7716aa71a2d0d118ca2583790.pdf?_ga=2.159537341.1857147401.1556717251-847747019.1556717251. Extracted December 2018.

Prutting, Carol A. (1982). Pragmatics as Social Competence. *Journal of Speech and Hearing Disorders*. 47, 123-134. Retrieved from: https://pubs.asha.org/doi/pdf/10.1044/jshd.4702.123.

Robbins, Joanne, Diez Gross, Roxann, Langmore, Susan, Lazarus, Cathy L., Martin Harris, Bonnie, McCabe, Daniel, Musson, Nan, Rosenbek, John C. (2008). Swallowing and Dyshagia. *Journal of Speech, Language, and Hearing Research*. 51, S276-S300. Retrieved from: https://pubs.asha.org/doi/pdf/10.1044/1092-4388%282008/021%29.

Robertson, Shari. Imagine Better-Imagine More! (2019) *The ASHA Leader*. 24, 6-7. Retrieved from: https://leader.pubs.asha.org/doi/10.1044/leader.FTP.24032019.6

Ropp, Thomas. (2017). 12 Ways to Unlock the Powers of the Vagus Nerve. Retrieved from: https://upliftconnect.com/12-ways-unlock-powers-vagus-nerve/.

Rosenberg, Stanley. (2017). *Assessing the Healing Power of the Vagus Nerve*. Berkeley, CA: North Atlantic Books.

Rothi, Leslie J. Gonzalez, Musson, Nan, Rosenbeck, John C., Sapienza, Christine M. (2008). Neuroplasticity and Rehabilitation Research for Speech, Language, and Swallowing Disorders. *Journal of Speech, Language, and Hearing Research.* 51, S222-S224. Retrieved from: https://pubs.asha.org/doi/10.1044/1092-4388%282008/017%29.

Seeman, Scott and Sims, Rebecca. Comparison of Psychophysiological and Dual-Task Measurement of Listening Effort. (2015). *Journal of Speech, Language, and Hearing Research.* 2015. 58, ,1781-1792. Retrieved from: https://pubs.asha.org/doi/10.1044/2015_JSLHR-H-14-0180.

Serafini, Giuseppe, Kaleagasioglu, Ferda, Mendolicchio, Leonardo, Norman, Rich and Conte, Elio. (2017). The Transcutaneous Vagus Nerve Stimulation Output of the NuCalm Device of Solace Lifesciences Is Found to Be a Multifractal and Therefore It Is Indicated in the Treatment of Heart Rate Variability in the Dysfunction of Autonomic Nervous System in Anxiety, Depression and Stress. *Journal of Behavioral and Brain Science.* 7, 532-543. Retrieved from: https://www.scirp.org/journal/PaperInformation.aspx?PaperID=80458.

Singh-Curry, Victoria and Husain, Masud. (2009). The Functional Role of the Inferior Parietal Lobe in the Dorsal and Ventral Stream Dichotomy. *Neuropsychologia.* 47, 1434-1448.Retrieved from: https://www.ncbi.nlm.nih.gov/pmc/articles/PMC2697316/.

Stevens, Anthony. (1994) *JUNG: A Very Short Introduction.* Oxford, New York: Oxford University Press. (Republished as *Jung: A Very Short Introduction* in 2001).

Stromberg, Joseph. (2015). This is what your brain looks like during an orgasm. *Vox.* Retrieved from: https://www.vox.com/2015/4/1/8325483/orgasms-science.

Thomas, Lisa B., Stemple, Joseph C., Andreatta, Richard D., Andrade, Francisco, H.(2009). Establishing a New Animal Model for the Study of Laryngeal Biology and Disease: An Anatomical Study of the Mouse Larynx. *Journal of Speech, Language, and Hearing Research*, 52, 802-811. Retrieved from: https://pubs.asha.org/doi/10.1044/1092-4388%282008/08-0087%29.

Travis, Lee Edward, Tuttle, W.W., Cowa, Donald W. (1936). A Study of Heart Rate during Stuttering. *Journal of Speech Disorders.* 1, 21-26. Retrieved from: https://pubs.asha.org/doi/10.1044/jshd.0101.21.

Turkstra, Lyn, Ciccia, Angela, Seaton, Christine. (2003). Interactive Behaviors in Adolescent Conversation Dyads. *Speech, Language, and Hearing Services in Schools.* 34:117-127. Retrieved from: https://doi.org/10.1044/0161-1461(2003/010)

The Free Dictionary. Retrieved from: https://www.thefreedictionary.com/vagotonic.

Van Riper, Charles. (1971). *The Nature of Stuttering.* Englewood Cliffs, N.J.: Prentice Hall-Inc.

Vinsen, Betsy Partin. (1999). *Language Disorders Across the Lifespan.* San Diego, CA: Singular Publishing Group, Inc.

Wallace, B. Alan. (2007). *Contemplative Science: Where Buddhism and Neuroscience Converge.* New York: N.Y.: Columbia University Press.

Walusknki, Oliver. (2006). Yawning: unsuspected avenue for a better understanding of arousal and interoception. *Medical Hypothesis.* 67, 6-14. Retrieved from: https://www.sciencedirect.com/science/article/pii/S0306987706000600.

Washington, Danni. "Xploration Nature Knows Best Concussion Collar Segment." Retrieved from: https://www.youtube.com/watch?v=q_Z3VdoWPIE.

Watson. Linda R., Baranek, Grace. T., Roberts, Jane E., Fabian, David J. and Perryman, Twyla Y. (2010). Behavioral and Physiological Responses to Child-Directed Speech as Predicators of Communication Outcomes in Children With Autism Spectrum Disorders. *Journal of Speech, Hearing, and Language Research.* 53, 1052-1064. Retrieved from: https://doi.org/10.1044/1092-4388(2009/09-0096).

Webster's New World Dictionary: Fifth Edition. (2018). Boston, New York: Houghton Mifflin Harcourt.

Wicker, Bruno, Keysers, Christian, Plailly, Jane, Royet, Hean-Pierre, Gallese Vittoria, Giacamo, Rizzolatti. (2003). *Both of Us Disgusted in My Insula*: *The Common Neural Basis of Seeing and Feeling Disgust.* Neuron. 40:655-664). Retrieved from: https://www.sciencedirect.com/science/article/pii/S0896627303006792.

Wilson-Pauwels, Linda, Akesson, Elizabeth J., Stewart, Patricia A. (1988). *Cranial Nerves: Anatomy and Clinical Comments.* Philadelphia, PA: B.C. Decker, Inc.

Wikipedia. Retrieved from: https://en.wikipedia.org/wiki/Ethology.

Wikipedia. Retrieved from: https://en.wikipedia.org/wiki/Reflex_syncope.

Wong, Patrick, Uppunda, Ajith, Parrish, Todd, and Dhar, Sumitrajit. The Cortical Mechanism of Speech Perception in Noise. (2008). *Journal of Speech, Language, and Hearing Research*. 51, 1026-1041.Retrieved from: https://pubs.asha.org/doi/10.1044/1092-4388%282008/075%29.

THE AUTHOR

Dorothy Bohntinsky, M.A., CCC-SLP, D.Min., has practiced as a speech-language pathologist (SLP) in clinical settings since 1976. She was Director of Speech Pathology and Audiology at Alameda County Medical Center from 1980 to 2002. She retired early and has since worked in a variety of settings including home health, skilled nursing, and Rehab Without Walls. She has been the per diem SLP in a long-term acute hospital that specializes in remediating respiratory failure since 2002.

Her personal journeys through family loss in 2000 and 2001 inspired her to pursue a doctorate in ministry and interfaith ordination in order to help communicatively impaired individuals and their families strengthen resilience. She graduated with her D.Min. from Wisdom University in San Francisco and graduated from and was ordained through the Chaplaincy Institute for Interfaith Ministries Berkeley in 2006.

Married since 1971, she lives in Hayward, California with her husband, Chuck. Besides being involved with her three young grandchildren, she enjoys gardening, home improvement projects, acrylic/oil painting, Native American rock art, writing, golf, and being a tai chi student. Dr. Bohntinsky's passion for exploring ways that the theory of Nonverbal Language Integration (NvLI) can be researched and applied within the fields of healthcare and education and shared with the general public continues to grow.

She has published three other books, which are on Amazon:
The Healing Room: Discovering Joy through the Journal (2002).
Transformational Healing through the Integration of Self (2006 doctoral dissertation published in 2016).
Sustenance: Integrating Creativity with Rock Art (2017).
She has a paper published, "A Rock Art Dilemma: To Chatter or Not to Chatter," in *American Indian Rock Art*, 2019, Volume 45 by the American Rock Art Research Association.

If you would like to learn more about the theory of NvLI, please go to the Institute of Nonverbal Language Integration at nonverballangaugeintegration.com. From there, you can contact Dr. Bohntinsky regarding individual and group training.

INDEX

A

Accessory nerve, 36, 37
Adaptive 13, 36
Adrenalin, 26, 63, 83, 84, 87
    Beta-adrenergic response, 25
    Adrenergic stimulation, 25
Abdominal viscera, 25, 35, 36
Afferent, 19, 23, 35, 36, 42, 58, 68
Agents of change, 43-44
Akesson, Elizabeth J., 38
Ali, Asif, 26
Alameda County Medical Center, 13, 78
American Speech-Language-Hearing
    Association (ASHA, 9, 13, 29, 30, 48,
    58, 63, 65, 74, 95, 96, 105,
    Code of Ethics, 75
    Peer Review Procedures, 107
    Scope of Practice, 7
Anderson, Raymond, E, 56
Andrew, James, vii
Andrew, Mary, vii
Animal research, 1, 2, 13
Apel, Ken, 75
Aphasia, 28, 29, 51, 62, 69
Apple, Charles. G, 32
Assessment, 18, 63, 65, 71, 81
Attention, 2, 6, 7, 9, 10, 16, 19, 21, 22, 24,
    26, 29, 42, 47, 48, 50, 52, 60, 61, 65,
    66, 71, 78, 79, 80, 87, 88, 89, 93, 97, 98,
    104
Audiologist, 63, 74, 75, 81, 95
Auditory nerve, 16
Auricular branch of the vagus nerve, 26
Autonomic nervous system, 24-27, 36, 37,
    39, 41-43, 50, 58, 62, 63, 66-68, 78, 82-
    84
    Commingled, 67, 105
    Parasympathetic, 25, 27, 34-37, 41-
    43, 56, 63, 66, 78, 82-83, 106
    Sympathetic, 19, 29, 32, 45, 52
    "Animal," 67
    "Vegetative," 67
    Three branches, 67

Autism, 66
Awareness, 13, 16-18, 22, 24, 30, 31, 34,
    41, 43, 52, 59, 62, 78, 82, 92, 114, 115
    Visual, 21-22
Aydogdu, Ibrahim, 61-62

B

Barnlund, Dean, 44
Behavior, 51, 52, 53, 54, 55, 58, 59, 61
    Behavioral change, 58,
    Behavioral regulation, 59
    Maladaptive, 39
    Motor, 58, 61
    Nonverbal, 60, 61
    Sensorimotor, 61
Big horn sheep, 2
Biobehavioral, 37, 41
Biomechanics, 57
Biomimicry, 2, 13
Bite, 18, 42
Blood pressure, 8, 14, 25, 26, 28, 30, 39,
    40, 50, 53, 59, 103, 109
Blood volume, 15
Bohntinsky, Dorothy, 42
Body language, 13, 73, 78, 83
Bolus, 18, 35, 62, 70
Boone, Daniel, 74
Bradycardia, 61, 66
Brain, 2, 3, 5, 6, 9, 11, 15, 18, 21, 23, 25-
    31, 34, 36, 37, 41, 42, 45-49, 51, 52, 57-
    62, 67, 82, 83, 96, 103, 104
    Diencephalon, 46
    Supratentorial brain, 46
    Brodmann's (area 7), 47
Brainstem, 46, 49, 59, 60, 62
Breath, 58, 74
Breathing, 68, 69, 71
Broca, Pierre Paul, 49
Buddhism, 47

C

Carotid artery, 2
Cavanna, Andrea, 37

Central regulatory features, 68
Certificate of Clinical Competence, 75
Cervix, 67
Christensen, Stephanie, 68, 69
Chowdhary, S., 24, 25, 37
Ciccia, Angela, 32
Cincinnati Children's Hospital, 3, 5, 6
Chaplaincy Institute for Interfaith
Ministries, 7, 53
CIAO, 8
Cognitive, 15, 16, 29, 47-49, 51, 52, 69, 70, 72, 81, 82, 85-86
    Exercises (See Exercises)
Cognitive language therapy, 86
Collar, 3-10, 8, 13, 14-16, 19, 21, 22, 24, 26, 28, 29, 31, 40, 42, 43, 48, 52, 54, 55, 59, 60, 62, 70, 71, 95,
    Neuro Shield, 3, 6, 9, 11, 23, 35, 37
    J Collar, 11-13, 15, 16
    Q Collar, 1, 9, 11, 13, 18, 23, 45, 54, 57, 78, 104, 111, 112,
Collins, J.J., 67
Commingle (See autonomic nervous system)
Communication, 7, 8, 16, 28, 31, 41, 48, 49, 51, 53, 54, 63, 65, 74, 76, 77, 79, 106, 115,
    Interpersonal, 32, 33, 38, 40, 44, 51, 56, 71, 76, 83, 108
    Intrapersonal, 53, 97
Compensatory strategies, 61, 70
Compression, 2-6, 13-17, 19, 22-24, 26, 31, 40, 43, 45, 52, 54, 55, 57, 59, 60, 62, 70, 71, 95, 114
Concentration, 11, 17
Concussion, 1-3, 6, 111
Consonants, 35, 82, 90
Contagious, 46, 47, 79,
Conte, Sergio, 26
Contemplation, 28, 30, 43,
Cough, 18, 26, 34, 89
Cranial nerves, 59
    CNV, VII, IX, X, XI, XII, 59
    CNV (see Trigeminal nerve)
    CNVII (see Facial nerve)
    CNVIII (see Auditory nerve)
    CNIX (see Glossopharyngeal)
    CNX (see Vagus nerve)
    CNXI (see Accessory nerve)
    CNXII (see Hypoglossal)

Counseling, 63
Crossman, A.R., 33-36, 49, 55,

D
Darley, Frederick, 33-35
Davidson, Richard, 28, 59
Deductive reasoning, 47
Deductive research design, 75
Diaphragm, 7, 23, 34, 36, 41, 46,
DiCesare Christopher, 4-5
Digastric muscle, 34
Documentation, 63, 81
Dopamine, 59
Durant, Kevin, 73
Dysphagia, 9, 35, 45, 56, 58, 60, 61, 95, 96, 98-100
    Therapy, 35, 56, 58, 60

E
Effort, 7, 21, 22, 29, 42
Efficacy research, 74
Eisenberg, Rita, 16
Electrocardiograms, 69
Electrophysiological, 46, 62
Electrical stimulation, 8, 26-27, 31
Elson, Lawrence, 34-36
Emotion, 7, 8, 26, 29-31, 40-43, 48-51, 54, 55, 61, 63, 66, 73, 77, 79, 81, 83, 100, 115
Emotional awareness, 13
Emotional balance, 24
Emotional regulation, 40
Emotionality, 69
Empathy, 6, 47, 48, 52, 84, 104
Enlightenment, 30
Enriched environments, 60, 61, 66
Epilepsy, 31
Eppinger, Hans, 5, 61, 63, 66-67, 107
Episodic memory (see memory)
Ertekin, Cumhum, 46-47, 57, 61-62
Esophagus, 17
Ethology, 13-14, 109
Ethnographic research designs, 75
Evidence-based practice, 72, 75-76
Executive functions, 54-55
Exercises, 3, 30-31, 40, 43, 45, 46, 48, 51, 52, 61-63, 68, 71, 81-82, 84, 95, 96-99, 102, 103, 105, 106-109

Exercises: Cognitive
  Cues, 90
  Imagery, 90
  Metaphors, 91
Exercises: Motor
  Articulation, 94-95
  Facial expression, 86-87
  Non-speech vocalizations, 88
  Oral movements, 87
  Posturing, 86
  Prosody, 90
Exercises: Progressive Vagus Nerve
  Activation, 87-89
Exercises: Sensory,
  Tactile, 95-96
Eyes
  Gaze, 7, 22, 71, 72, 86
  Glance, 72
  Lateral (left/right), 71-72, 86

F

Facial expression, 8, 22, 31, 37, 46, 50, 53,
  62, 77-80, 82, 84, 102, 106
  Exercises, (See exercises)
Facial feedback hypothesis, 79
Facial nerve (CN VII), 34-35
Fight/flight, 22 37, 41-43, 49, 72, 83-84,
  87
Fluency, 7, 70
Fogel, Alan, 21, 33, 37
Foley, Gilbert, 43, 44
Fractal geometry, 27
  Monofractals, 27
  Multifractals, 27
Franca, Jessica, 27
Frequencies , 16, 34, 77
  Low, 16-17, 50
  High, 16-17, 50
Friel-Patti, Sandy, 74-75
Furchgott, R. F., 26

G

Gag reflex, 35, 70
Gasp, 7, 90, 93
Geller, Elaine, 43, 44
Genioglossus muscle, 58
Gick, Bryan, 57-58
Giuliano, F., 67
Glance (see Eyes)

Glossopharyngeal nerve (CNIX), 17, 33,
  35, 37
Goal, 5, 14, 19, 22, 30, 58, 62, 82, 84, 92,
  103, 104, 107
Goleman, Daniel, 28
Grandchildren, 11-12, 14, 15, 19, 21, 30,
  72-73, 103
Greenstein, Adam, 42, 49-50
Greenstein, Ben, 42, 49-50
Guidelines, 75, 81-84
Gudmundsson, Garner, 23, 38

H

Habib, Safia, 26
Harper, Robert, 72, 77, 78
Harryman, Elizabeth, 32
Head, 33, 36-37, 39, 40, 41, 48, 54, 61, 62,
  65, 67, 70, 71, 73, 80, 87, 88,91, 92, 93,
  96, 102, 109
Head injury, 1-2, 9, 13, 16
Health, 27, 29, 30, 31, 34, 36, 39, 40, 43,
  46, 61, 63, 66, 67, 68, 80, 83, 104, 105
Healthcare, 1, 8, 18, 39, 107, 108,
Hearing, 7, 13, 16, 46, 50, 68, 101, 102,
  108, 109
Heart, 23, 25, 26, 27, 35, 36, 40, 41, 59, 61,
  62, 67, 68, 86, 89
Heart rate, 69-70, 99
  Stuttering, 69-70
Heart rate variability (HRV), 26, 27, 61,
  63, 66, 68-69
Helou, Leo, 9
Hess, Leo, 5, 61, 63, 66-67, 104
Hierarchical, 43, 85
Holland, Audrey, vii
Homeostasis, 23, 24, 26, 28, 30-31, 41, 43,
  58, 63, 70, 71, 73, 76, 80, 83-84, 85, 87,
  96, 97, 99, 104-105, 111, 114, 115
Hormones, 46
Humbert, Ianessa, 15, 17-18, 60
HRV (see heart rate variability)
Huether, Sue, 25
Hyoid bone, 34, 54, 57-58, 62
Hypertension, 24-25
Hyolaryngeal excursion, 58
Hypogastric nerve, 67
Hypothalamus, 26, 46, 49, 52, 68
Hypothesis, 6-7, 11, 15, 19, 21, 24, 31, 49,
  50-51, 55, 71, 74

I

Iacoboni, Marco, 79
Imagery, 47-48, 72, 82,
    Exercises (See Exercises)
Imagination, 56, 67, 72, 82, 95, 98, 105
Imaginologist, 95
Immobilization, 43, 49, 80, 83-84, 87, 114
Imprinting, 13
Inner mirroring, 79
Innerro, L. J., 26
Infrahyoid muscles, 62
Innate releasing mechanisms, 117-118
Innervate, 6, 9, 19, 22, 26, 31, 34-35, 43,
    47-48, 50, 54, 57-58, 62, 72, 70-73, 79-
    80, 81-82, 85, 87, 100, 114
Inotropic responses, 25
Inspiration (see Respiration)
Interoception, 21
Interpersonal, 32, 33
Intervention, 73-76, 81, 96, 104
Intuition, 55

J

Jaw, 34, 42, 46, 90
Jones, Theresa, 21, 29-30, 61
Jugular foramen, 23, 36-37, 57
Jugular vein, 2-3, 5-6, 9, 11, 14, 15-19, 23-
    24, 31, 37, 57, 114
Jung, Carl, 111, 113-114

K

Kapit, Wynn, 34-35
Kegels, 67-68, 93
Kimiko Abe, 45, 57
Kleim, Jeffery, 21, 29, 61
Kok, Bethany, 61, 66
Kresheck, Janet, 32
Kurkland, Jacquie, 51, 53

L

Language, 7, 16, 18, 51, 53, 65, 68, 78, 86,
95, 98, 100
L-arginine, 25
Larynx, 3, 6-7, 9-10, 17-19, 22-23, 33-36,
46, 54, 55, 57, 58, 60-62
    Intrinsic musculature, 9-10
Learning, 13, 16, 21, 27-29, 33, 43, 50-51,
    55, 58-59, 61, 63, 65-66, 76, 80, 82-84,
    96-97, 104-106

LeDoux, Joseph, 57, 59, 103-104
Lemire, Joe, 2-3, 57
Limbic system, 26, 49, 50, 55
    Amygdala, 49, 63
    Cingulate gyrus, 48-50
    Circuit of Papez, 49-50
    Hypothalamus, 26, 46, 49, 52, 68
Linguistic anxiety, 28
Listening, 34, 48-50, 68, 79, 92, 97
Loler, J. M., 68
Lorenz, Konrad, 11, 13
Loss, 7-8, 24, 30, 49, 53, 83, 110
Love-Sudduth, Debbie, 107, 109, 113
Lower motor neurons, 47

M

Magnetic Resonance Imaging, 6, 47
Maladaptive, (See Behavior)
Mandible, 34
Martin, Ruth E., 460
Masseter muscle, 34
Mastication, 46
Mandelbrot, Benoit, 27
McCance, Kathryn, 23, 25
Medulla, 25
Mehrabian, Albert, 77, 86
Mehrabian equation, 77
Memory, 13, 16, 29, 45, 51, 52, 55, 80, 97
    Episodic, 47, 49
Mendelsohn maneuver, 60-61
Metabolism, 52
Metaphor, 18, 62, 72, 79, 82
    Exercises (See Exercises)
Mindfulness, 48, 53-54
Mirror neurons, 79
Mobilization, 37
Modulators, 59, 68
Monoamines, 59
Monro-Kellie doctrine, 23-24
Mood, 5, 7, 8-10, 14, 15-19, 22-24, 25, 29,
    31, 37, 42, 55, 60-61, 71-72, 111-112,
    114-115
Moore, Lisa, 104
Mortensen, David, 56, 79
Mosik, Scott Reid, 57-58
Motivation, 63
Motor, 6-7, 16-17, 23, 25, 33-37, 39-41,
    43, 47, 51, 58, 60-63, 67-68, 70-72, 78-
    79, 81-82, 85, 97, 100, 102

Motor exercises, 87-90
Murid, F, 26
Mylohyoid muscle, 34

N
Neary, D, 33-36, 49, 55
Neck, 2-3, 8-13, 17-19, 21-24, 26, 31, 35-
    37, 40, 42-43, 45-46, 48, 54-55, 57-59,
    61-63, 67, 70-72, 86-89, 91, 96, 98-
    100, 103, 105
Nervana, 31
Neuroception, 43
Neurochemicals, 52
Neuromodulator, 25
Neuromuscular modules, 5, 8, 58
Neurophysiology, 6, 19, 46, 44, 76, 114
Neuroplasticity (neural plasticity), 28-29,
    56, 58-62, 76, 106, 115
Neurotransmitters, 45, 52
Neuro Shield (see Collar)
Newberg, Andrew, 6, 30, 45, 47, 50, 52-
    53, 63
Nicolosi, Lucille, 32, 56
Nitric oxide, 23-25, 45, 55
Nitrous oxide, 23-24
Non-verbal
    Behaviors, 31, 71-73, 77, 80, 82, 84,
        107, 113-115
    Exercises (See Exercises)
    Language, 8, 53, 55, 58-62, 70, 74, 76-
        77, 80, 81-82, 84, 95, 104-107
        Negative connotations, 71, 73, 78, 84
        Vocalizations, 41, 58, 77-79, 82, 89-91
Nonverbal Language Integration Theory,
    51, 61, 74, 76, 79-80, 82-83, 85, 102-
    106, 107-109, 114-115
Nose, 21, 86-88, 91-92, 102
    Nares, 22, 42
    Nostrils, 21-22, 24, 26, 28-29, 31, 42,
        48, 51, 54-55, 58, 61, 107
NuCalm tVNS system, 26-27
Nucleus ambiguus, 36, 70

O
Oculomotor cranial nerve, 42
Omohyoid muscle, 2-3, 5-6, 9-10, 13, 45,
    55-56, 57-58, 60, 62, 110
Oral Movement Exercises, 89-91
Ordination, 18, 30, 79
Orienting, 65

Outcomes, 26, 29, 43, 51-55, 61-63, 66,
    71-72, 76, 81-82, 95-96, 103-106, 113-
    115
Oxytocin, 52

P
Palmer, John, 34-35, 57
Palpate, 34, 42, 55
Palatopharyngeal, 70
Papez, James, 49
    Circuit of Papez, (see limbic system)
Paralinguistics, 77
    Emphasis, 77
    Intonation (inflections/shifts), 77-78
    Pauses, 77-78
    Stress, 77
Parietal lobe, 45-48, 50
Pathways, 29, 31, 34, 39, 41, 43, 47, 49,
    58, 65, 68, 70,
    (See Vagus Nerve Pathways)
Pelletier, Cathy, 17
Pelvic nerves, 67
Personality, 59
Phenotypic, 5
Phylogenic, 45, 79
Pheumograph, 69
Phylogenetic, 16, 22, 49, 78
Pitch, 17-18, 33, 57, 65, 71, 74, 77-78, 99-
    100
Polyvagal Theory, 36-37, 39-43, 65, 79,
    83, 97-102, 114
Pompon, Rebecca Hunting, 28-30
Porges, Stephen, 36-38, 39-43, 49, 50, 61,
    63, 66, 68, 79, 83
Posture, 5-6, 31, 37, 40, 53, 55, 72-73, 77-
    78, 82, 84, 102, 106, 108
    Exercises (See Exercises)
Placebo, 16, 24
Platek, S.M, 47
Pragmatics, 59, 61-62, 71, 76, 77-79, 113-
    114
Precuneus, 45, 47-48, 72, 82, 98
Productive, 21
Profanity, 78
Pudendal nerve, 67
Prutting, Carol, 77

Q
Q Collar (See collar)
Quantality, 57-58

R

Rams, 2
Rapport, vii, 40, 42-44, 55-56, 61, 63, 72, 74, 76, 78-82, 105-106, 115-116
Reciprocity, 72, 79
Rehabilitation, 1, 29, 59, 95
Relationship-based interventions, 43-44
Relaxation, 8, 22, 26, 30-31, 34, 62, 87, 92, 99
Respiration, 45, 50-51, 54, 62
   Inspiration, 46, 57-58, 60, 66, 69
   Expiration, 46, 69
Respiratory, 25, 36, 46, 47, 66, 69,
   Arrhythmia (RSA), 61, 66, 68
   RSA and social competence, 66
Rest/digest, 66
Restoration, 39, 43, 63, 80
Robbins, Joanne, 58
Robertson, Sheri, 95
Ropp, Thomas, 31
Rosenberg, Stanley, 1, 31, 33-37, 43, 45, 51, 70-72

S

Saliva, 21, 35, 45-47, 50
Seaton, Christine, 32
Seeman, Scott, 68
Self, Trisha, 75
Semantics, 53
Sensory, 7, 15, 18-19, 21, 23, 26, 29, 33-36, 41-42, 48, 51, 58, 60, 62, 78-79, 81-82, 86, 91
   Exercises (See Exercises)
Sensory integration, 17, 60, 62, 79, 104
Sexual arousal, 67
Sexual intercourse, 69
Sigh, 17, 45, 71, 73-74, 86-87, 93, 99
Sims, Rebecca, 20, 68
Smith, David, 2
Slosh, 3, 5, 114
Sneeze, 3, 9, 34, 86, 90, 93
Social competence, 66, 77
Social engagement, 33-34, 39-42, 47, 57, 71, 73, 76, 79-80, 82-84, 104, 106, 113
Socioemotional competence, 32
Soft palate, 17, 35
Somatomotor, 39-40
Spinal cord, 60
Spinal cord injury, 67

Speech, 7, 9, 13, 16, 31-34, 36, 38, 48, 49-50, 54, 58, 59, 62-63, 68-70, 72, 74, 77-78, 86, 97, 100-101
   Child-directed speech (baby talk), 65
Speech-language pathologist (SLP), 1, 3, 5-8, 12, 20, 33, 40, 54, 70, 72, 74-75, 78, 81, 9552, 57, 59, 62, 64, 67
Speech-language therapy, 53, 76
Speech-language pathology, 7-8, 59, 63, 65, 77, 107
Stapedius, 34
Stimulus-response theory, 68
Sternohyoid muscle, 57
Stewart, Patricia A., 38
Stress, 7-8, 22, 25-31, 33-34, 37, 39-40, 45, 51-52, 55, 58, 63, 68, 71, 73, 77-80, 82-83, 92
Stromberg, Joseph, 67
Stuttering, 40, 69-70
   Avoidances, 70
   Interruptor devices, 70
Subjective self-reporting, 69
Swallow, 3, 7, 9, 16,-18, 1-22, 97, 36, 40-41, 45-46, 50, 54, 56, 557-63, 80, 87, 105
   Dry, 21
   Rest, 46
   Phases, 62
Swallowing therapy, 18, 46
Synapses, 59, 70

T

Task, 6, 9, 12, 16, 21, 29, 47, 51, 54, 69, 81, 101, 108
Taste buds, 17, 25, 60
Temporalis muscle, 34
Temporal coupling, 46
Tensor tympani, 34
Thalamus, 33-34, 46, 48-49
Theory, 5, 6, 14, 17, 35, 45, 47, 51, 68, 74-76, 79, 81, 97
   (See Nonverbal Language Integration Theory)
   (See Polyvagal Theory)
Thomas, Clayton, 25
Thoracic, 23, 35-36
Throat, 8-9, 11-12, 18, 21, 28, 54, 66, 70, 86, 90-91, 93
Tiling, 12
Tool, 27, 37, 43, 45, 47, 84, 111

Tongue, 2, 17, 18-19, 21-22, 34-36, 58, 60-61, 70, 87, 97
Tongue map, 17
Townsend, J.N., 24-25, 37
Travis, Lee Edward, 69-70
Traits, 13, 28, 59
Trigeminal Nerve, 33, 62
Trimble, Michael, 47
Turkstra, Lyn, 32

U
Uplift, 31
Uterus, 67

V
Vagotonia, 25, 65-66
Vagal activity, 25, 65-66
Vagal brake, 37, 63
Vagal tone, 54, 58, 68
Vagus nerve, 17-19, 21, 23-32, 33, 35-37, 41, 43, 48, 50, 52-53, 61-63, 65-68, 70-74, 81, 84, 93, 95-96, 103, 105, 107
    Branches:
    Dorsal Vagus, 36-37, 41, 43, 60, 79, 83, 87, 114
    Ventral branch, 36-37, 41-43, 45, 50-51, 53-55 58, 62, 70-74, 79-80, 82-83, 85-87, 92, 104, 106, 107, 112-115
    Auricular branch, 26
    Activation of, 19, 50, 71, 80, 82, 85, 87, 100, 115
    Afferents, 19, 23, 35-36, 42, 58, 68
    Efferents, 17, 23, 25, 36, 39, 49, 68
    Electrical stimulation of, 26-27, 31
    Exercises (See Exercises)
    Indirect vagal effect, 25
    Pathways, 17, 17, 23, 26, 31, 41, 45, 55, 65, 70, 71, 74, 78, 79-80, 82-87, 93, 95-96, 104, 114-115
Van Riper, Charles, 65, 70
Valsalva, 65, 70, 91
Venting behaviors, 78-80
Verbal expression, 70
Verbal reasoning, 72-73
Visceral efferent, 36, 39
Visceromotor, 40
Visual cues, 85, 101,
VitalStim Therapy, 8
Vocal cords, 54, 57
Voice therapy, 3, 6, 16, 18, 51

Voice quality, 70-71, 74
Volition, 56
Vowels, 3, 35, 57, 74, 82, 90
"Vox" article, 67

W
Waldman, 6, 30, 45, 47, 50, 52-53, 63
Wallace, Alan, 47-48
Washington, Danni, 6, 12, 37, 54, 112
Watson, Linda, 65-66
Wellbeing, 27, 30-31, 59, 74, 105
Wellness, 34, 63, 82-84, 104
Wernicke's area, 48
White coat anxiety, 8, 18, 39, 113
Wilson-Pauwels, Linda, 38
Wisdom, 54
Wisdom University, 7, 53, 113
Woodpecker, 2
Wong, Patrick, 48, 50
Workload, 69
Wright, Heather Harris, 68-69

X
Xploration, 6, 12

Y
Yawn, 2-3, 5-7, 9-10, 17, 31, 37, 43, 45-52, 53-55, 57, 60, 62-63, 67, 71, 78, 81, 82, 87, 93, 103
    Culture, 73
    Eliciting the swallow, 46
    Phases of, 46
    Reasons to yawn, 52
    Yawn/Sigh voice therapy strategy, 74

NOTES

www.ingramcontent.com/pod-product-compliance
Lightning Source LLC
Chambersburg PA
CBHW082357270326
41935CB00013B/1658